LIVING
IN
POLAR
REGIONS

LIVING IN POLAR REGIONS

A CULTURAL GEOGRAPHY

THEODORE A. REES CHENEY

FRANKLIN WATTS | 1987
NEW YORK | LONDON | TORONTO | SYDNEY

11094

Maps by Vantage Art, Inc.

Cover photographs courtesy of Alaska Division of Tourism (top left and bottom right); Ward Wells/Shostal Associates (top right); Fabian/Sygma (bottom left).

Photographs courtesy of © Stephen J. Krasemann/ Photo Researchers: p. 20; Alaska Division of Tourism: pp. 22, 28, 31, 40; © Arthur Tress/Photo Researchers: pp. 23 (top), 42; © Sam Kimura/Photo Researchers: p. 23 (bottom); © William Bacon III/Photo Researchers: p. 27; © Omikron/Photo Researchers: p. 30; © Paolo Koch/Photo Researchers: p. 33; Canadian Consulate General: pp. 35, 69, 70, 73, 75, 77; © Rychetnik/Photo Researchers: p. 36; © George Laycock/Photo Researchers: p. 39; Tass from Sovfoto: pp. 53, 54, 58, 60; Fabian/Sygma: p. 59; Richard Harrington/Photo Trends: p. 68; Quebec Tourism: p. 80.

Library of Congress Cataloging-in-Publication Data

Cheney, Theodore A. Rees
(Theodore Albert Rees), 1928–
Living in polar regions.

(A Cultural geography)
Bibliography: p.
Includes index.
Summary: Describes the characteristics of the world's polar regions and compares and contrasts the interrelationship of geography and culture of polar communities in three areas, the North Slope of Alaska, a valley in northeastern Siberia, and Hudson Bay in central Canada. Also discusses the work of cultural geographers.
1. Anthropo-geography—Arctic Regions—Juvenile literature. 2. Arctic Regions—Social life and customs—Juvenile literature. 3. Arctic Regions—Description and travel—Juvenile literature. [1. Anthropo-geography—Arctic Regions. 2. Arctic Regions—Social life and customs 3. Arctic Regions—Description and travel] I. Title. II. Series.
GF891.C44   1987   304.2'0911'3   85-26585
ISBN 0-531-10150-9

CONTENTS

TO EDDY WETALTUK OF
GREAT WHALE RIVER,
AND ALL THE OTHER SONS
AND DAUGHTERS OF THE
WORLD'S CIRCUMPOLAR LANDS

1

AN INTRODUCTION TO POLAR REGIONS

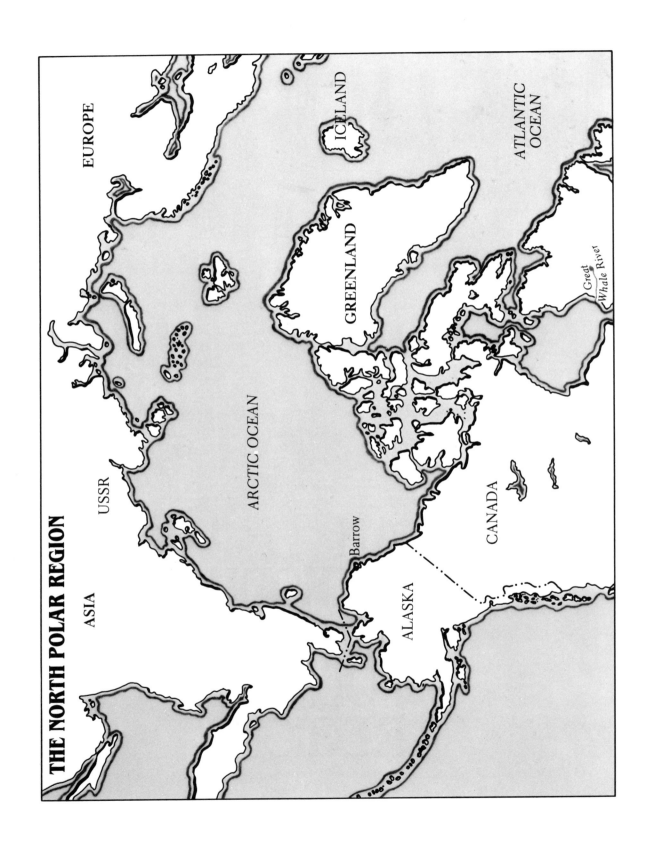

THE NORTH POLAR REGION

EUROPE

ICELAND

ATLANTIC OCEAN

GREENLAND

Great Whale River

ASIA

USSR

ARCTIC OCEAN

Barrow

CANADA

ALASKA

Picture yourself in a flowering meadow. As far as you can see, bright green plants hug the ground. Scattered across this green surface are red, yellow, and purple flowers. The sun is shining in the sky—but your watch says it's 2 a.m.! As you walk along, a family of birds flutters out of the wet plants, just in front of you. Their wings beat loudly in the quiet air. There are tents and a campfire nearby, and far in the distance you can make out the twinkling white peaks of high mountains.

Close your eyes and the scene changes. The thundering of hooves is all around as reindeer gallop past. As soon as they are gone, you feel the piercing cold through thick layers of fur clothing. The sky is a deep blue and there is no wind. There are small, stunted evergreen trees all around. Nearby, a helicopter is parked next to a tall, teepee-like tent.

Close your eyes once again and imagine another scene. You are in a small motorboat, and your navigator is cutting right next to a large chunk of floating ice. In fact, you are surrounded by big, jagged chunks. A light snow is falling. Suddenly, there is a loud splash in front of you, followed by snorting and puffing sounds. Your boat slows to a crawl so that you can watch the polar bear swim away from the noisy intruders.

You have just been to the North Slope of Alaska, to the Kolyma River valley in northeastern Siberia, and to Hudson Bay in central Canada. These three places are part of the world's north *polar* region,

the cold belt of land that rings the top of the world.

The world's polar regions have several things in common. These include:

Low precipitation levels—The air in the far north is cold and dry, so that little *precipitation* falls, either as rain or snow.

Frozen ground—Much of the polar region's soils are underlain by *permafrost*, permanently frozen ground, a few inches to a few feet below the surface.

Two major kinds of vegetation—The polar region is clothed either in dark green evergreens or low mosses and shrubs.

Low population density—People have lived in the Far North for thousands of years, but never in large numbers. Life there is difficult and unappealing to many people. Only in recent years have cities of any size begun to grow in polar regions.

Transportation challenges—The forests and lakes of the North have not made roadbuilding easy. Also, if roads are built on permafrost, they will buckle and collapse. Traditional travel by small boat and dogsled teams has been largely replaced by snowmobiles and airplanes. Roads and railroads are still in short supply.

An economy based on mining and timber—In the past, the native northerners lived off the land. Today, they and new settlers work in mining, the oil-drilling business, and logging. Much of these resources are transported for use by people who live far from the polar region.

Dependence on world systems—Even if polar communities are far away from most of the world's people, there are still strong ties between the Far North and the rest of the world. For example, oil companies have discovered that a lot of oil lies below the ocean floor, just offshore of northern Alaska. To extract this oil, giant camps and new towns have been built for new workers and equipment. Many *Inuit* and Indians have become skilled oil workers.

The oil industry has brought many changes to the native peoples and to the land they inhabit. No longer are the Inuit and Indians independent and self-sufficient. They have come to rely on the foods, tools, and entertainment of the larger North American society.

This book will compare and contrast the cultural geography of life in three different northern communities. In addition to learning about the polar region, you will learn about the art and science of geography. You will also learn how cultural geographers study regions and how they view the relationship between people and their natural environment.

WHAT IS CULTURAL GEOGRAPHY?

Cultural geographers study the interwoven lives of people and their environments. Cultural geographers ask such questions as: How did the people who live here get here? How did they decide where to settle and how to make a living? How have they influenced their environment (land and climate) and how has it affected them? A major focus of cultural geography is how *culture* and *environment* fit together. By environment we mean the physical fea-

tures of the world around us: the air, water, plant life, soils and rocks that make up the world's biosphere. The biosphere is the envelope of life surrounding the globe. Culture is a way of life devised by human beings for getting along with the environment and each other. It is made up of beliefs, knowledge, religion, technology, economy, art, science, medicine, and philosophy. These are just a few of the elements of a culture. People around the world have put these elements together in different ways to create many diverse cultures.

In this book, you will see that the Inuit, *Yakaghir*, and Cree Indians have created native cultures within the polar environment. In contrast, American, Russian, and Canadian settlers have brought their cultures from the outside world to the polar regions and are still learning how to live comfortably in the Far North.

HOW CULTURAL GEOGRAPHERS STUDY REGIONS

A *region* is an area within which elements of culture or environment are similar. Outside the region the elements are different. For example, if farmers in a certain area all grow the same crop, then you can draw a line around that area on a map and call it a region. Actually, though, regions are more complicated. A region is usually made up of several elements that overlap unevenly. For example, look at Figure 2. It is a map of the world in which rainfall and vegetation patterns overlap. It separates the world into regions based on rainfall and vegetation.

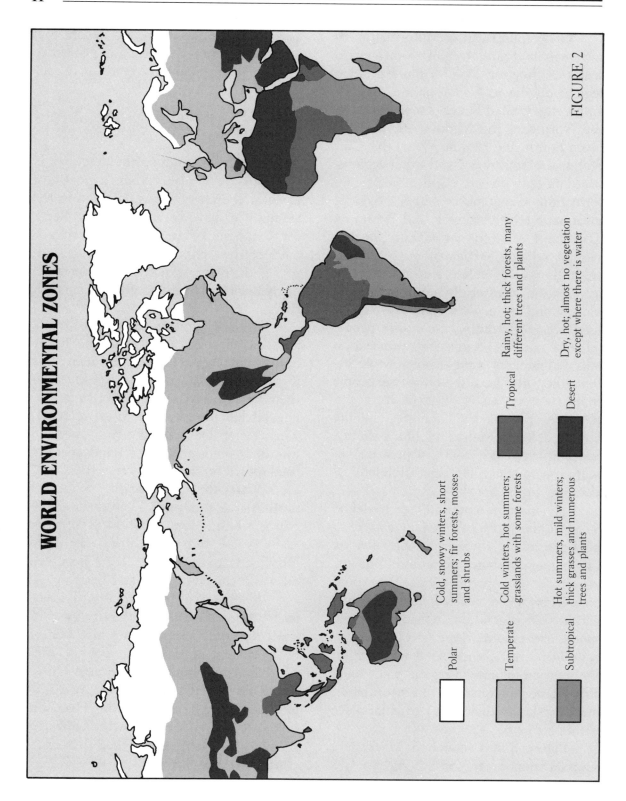

WORLD ENVIRONMENTAL ZONES

Polar — Cold, snowy winters, short summers; fir forests, mosses and shrubs

Temperate — Cold winters, hot summers; grasslands with some forests

Subtropical — Hot summers, mild winters; thick grasses and numerous trees and plants

Tropical — Rainy, hot; thick forests, many different trees and plants

Desert — Dry, hot; almost no vegetation except where there is water

FIGURE 2

Geographers can use information to map regions around the globe—on a world scale. Or they can look for more detailed regions on the scale of a nation. For example, the United States is separated into the Northeast, the Middle Atlantic, the Deep South, the Middle West, the Gulf States, the Southwest, and other regions, based on both objective and subjective information. Geographers gather objective information by observing and counting. This kind of information can include rainfall, religion, settlement patterns, and vegetation. Geographers gather subjective information by carefully noting what people say and do in their daily lives or by listening to or reading the stories people tell one another. Subjective information tells geographers what region people believe they live in and how these people think their region is different from surrounding places. For example, in the United States, a woman might say she is a Southerner because she has spent an important part of her life, her childhood, for example, in the South.

The more information used to define a region, the smaller the region is likely to be. For example, the world can be divided into big regions based on rainfall. But just imagine how many tiny regions you would have if, on top of rainfall, you laid down patterns of vegetation, religion, favorite sports, and favorite desserts! Cultural geographers must decide what information to use when defining a region. They must also decide how much of this information must overlap to include a particular place within a region.

Figure 3 is a *model*. A model is a simplification of the real thing. In this case it is a simplification of a region. Figure 3 shows how objective and subjective information overlap to form a region.

CULTURAL EXCHANGE IS THRIVING

The three polar communities described in this book are all places where a great deal of cultural exchange goes on. That is, the people who have lived in the Far North for hundreds of years have introduced parts of their culture to new arrivals. In return, the northern natives have accepted many things that newer settlers bring with them.

Cultural exchange can involve objects, customs, and beliefs. In Siberia, the natives now fly out to their reindeer herds in helicopters, a machine introduced to them by recent Russian arrivals. In return, new settlers have learned to eat reindeer, which once fed only the natives. Now hundreds of thousands of reindeer are a food source for new northern settlers.

What about the native people of north Alaska, the Inuit? They invented the parka, a basic piece of clothing worn by many people today. The Inuit also have introduced to non-Inuits their beautiful art works carved of bone and ivory.

What parts of the larger North American culture have entered the Inuit way of life? Not only objects, but also beliefs have influenced the Inuit way of life. Most religious Inuit have become Christians, moving away from their own religious outlook. They have also taken on many of the values of North American society—for example, the idea that competition is a good thing.

A MODEL OF A REGION

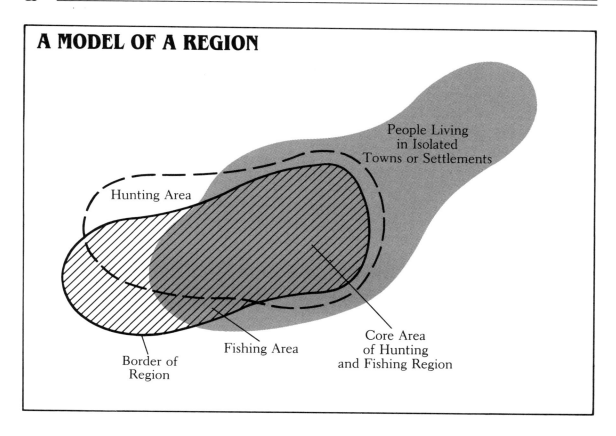

People Living
in Isolated
Towns or Settlements

Hunting Area

Core Area
of Hunting
and Fishing Region

Fishing Area

Border of
Region

HOW ENVIRONMENT AND CULTURE FIT TOGETHER

You may be asking yourself how environment and culture fit together in the world's polar region. First, the environment does not solely determine the type of culture in a region. That is, low temperatures, short summers, and frozen ground do not completely dictate how human beings live. If people were only controlled by their environment, then all people in all areas of the polar region around the world might be leading the same lives. But this is not so. Human choices and decision-making are

not solely at the mercy of the environment. However, neither does culture entirely control the environment. If people completely controlled the polar region's environment, then all people in all areas of the polar region might be leading very different lives. But this is not so, because we have seen that there are many similarities among northern communities in the way the land is used.

Culture and environment interact. That is, each influences the other. For example, Americans arriving in the frozen north decided they could improve on the dog team and sled as a method of transportation. So these new arrivals brought snowmobiles with them. Unlike sled dogs, these machines did not have to be fed or housed and never had to rest. It looked as if the snowmobile had conquered the environment. However, consider what happens if the snowmobile runs out of gas far from a settlement. Suddenly, the driver is at the mercy of the environment! If the driver had a hungry dog team, he would cut a hole in the ice and catch fish to feed them. But there is no gasoline on the *Arctic* ice. It looks as though the snowmobile is not so independent of nature after all.

There always has to be give and take between people and the environment they live in. In order to live comfortably in the North, both the natives and the new arrivals have to strike a balance between the life they would like to live and the resources available.

Some cultural geographers believe that the more a culture uses its natural resources, the greater the risk of natural disaster. For example, for hundreds of years, the Indian tribes of central Canada trapped the many fur-bearing animals and used them to make clothes, food, and tools. There were more than enough animals because Indian populations were low and the Indians were not interested in killing more animals than they could use.

Then the Europeans appeared with a different idea about fur-bearing animals. These men wanted the Indians to trap as many animals as they possibly could. The Europeans made the skins into hats and coats for the residents of distant European cities. The outsiders had no interest in the food value of these creatures. Within a few decades, the fur-bearing animals of eastern Canada had almost vanished, and the Europeans moved west to new areas.

It was then the Indians found themselves in trouble, for there were no longer enough beaver and otter for their own needs. This lack of food led to disease and starvation. It is clear that the Indians and Europeans had overused one of their most precious resources, with great suffering as a result.

When studying the world's polar region, cultural geographers may ask the following questions:

■ How have culture and environment interacted in this region?

■ How do people as children learn to use their environment?

■ If the culture or the environment changes, will these people be able to keep up with the changes?

■ How many families can the environment support?

■ If the culture changes, can the environment support more or fewer families?

■ How do people protect themselves from natural hazards, such as loss of a food source?

■ How successful or costly are their hazard-protection methods?

■ When two or more cultures meet, what items and beliefs are shared or traded?

As you study the world's polar region, you can ask similar questions. These questions also can help you learn more about the region you live in.

2

BARROW,
IN ALASKA

The twin-engine Otter plane slows as the pilot sees the village of Barrow coming into view to the south, right where Alaska meets the frozen Arctic Ocean. Even before he can see the flashing beacon lights, he knows the village is near by the thin layer of black smog on a white background that spreads over the sprinkling of houses and roads. The smog layer spreads to the northwest toward Point Barrow, where the military radar has been automatically tracking the small plane ever since it left the oil rig out on the frozen Beaufort Sea. The plane had taken off an hour earlier from an airstrip on the sea ice, not far from an oil rig, where a drilling crew lives and works in the subzero weather.

The plane is carrying mail from the drillers; also on board is an Inuit man, Joe Nageak, returning home to Barrow for a few days' vacation. Inuit is the native name for the Eskimo, the people who have occupied the frozen lands of the Arctic, that region of the earth that circles the North Pole for thousands of years. As he does every time he returns, Joe tells the pilot that he used to work for the Navy's Arctic Research Laboratory at Point Barrow. When the oil companies began drilling exploration holes all along the lands that slope north from the Brooks Range, he had very happily signed on to work for them. He couldn't resist five hundred dollars per week, plus free room and board, even though he knew it meant being away from his wife and children for two months at a time.

As the Otter's flaps are lowered and the plane drops through the smog layer toward the airstrip, pilot and passenger see several hundred small, brightly colored houses, dim in the darkness of a January noon. Barrow, the largest Inuit community in the world and the northernmost town in the United States, consists of about six city blocks. Of the town's 3,000 citizens, 2,700 are Inuit.

The plane's skis soon reach for the runway of packed snow. The plane taxis up to a group of snowmobiles parked outside the tiny terminal with the long name— Wiley Post–Will Rogers Airport. It was named in honor of the American aviator and the humorist, who both died in a small-plane crash in the Far North in 1935.

The pilot and Joe Nageak recognize their families' snowmobiles sitting outside the terminal, motors idling loudly. Fumes of carbon monoxide and other pollutants from these and hundreds of other snow machines (as Alaskans call them), trucks, taxis, and motorcycles rise up until they're stopped by a layer of heavy, colder air that forces the fumes to spread out into a thin layer of smog. Every arctic town that has many vehicles has a blanket of polluted air hanging above it during the long cold months. The cold climate makes things worse, because no one turns off gasoline motors for fear they won't start up again.

Joe's son, Andy, and daughter, Grace, greet him happily inside the terminal, and all three drive off on their two snow-mobiles. Father and son go directly home, while Grace drives over to pick up her mother, Faye, who works as a typist for the Inuit-owned Arctic Slope Corporation. Faye's boss realizes she's excited at having Joe home, and tells Faye to take the rest of the day off to celebrate.

THE PLACE

From the 3,000- to 9,000-foot (914- to 2,743-m) peaks of the Brooks Range, northern Alaska slopes downward, reaching out into the Arctic Ocean at Point Barrow. This arctic slope is a treeless, flat plain without hills or valleys. In the summer when the snow melts, there is water everywhere, floating on top of the permafrost, or frozen ground. A network of streams, lakes, and rivers covers the land's surface. This land, the *tundra*, is called a "frozen desert" because it receives less than 10 inches (25 cm) of moisture (either rain or snow) in a year.

The brief summer teems with plant and animal life. Mosses, flowers, grasses, sedges, and lichens cover the ground. Hare, squirrel, fox, ptarmigan, ducks, and geese inhabit this sunny world, and caribou are found in and near the mountains. For more than two months each year, there is twenty-four-hour sunshine. The ice pack retreats out to sea, freeing the shoreline for boat travel.

From September to May, snow covers the ground, frozen rivers are used as roads, and the region seems lifeless. From November 15, Barrow has seventy-two days without sun. Animals and humans retreat to small, snug places.

Temperatures

Low temperatures present many challenges to those who live in the North. In northern Alaska yearly temperatures average around 10° above zero Fahrenheit (−12° C). For about half of the days of the year—more than 170—the temperature is 0° F or below. Each winter the Arctic Ocean freezes to a depth of 5 to 10 feet (150–300 cm). Only the most powerful icebreaking ships can reach a place like Barrow in winter. The ground is permanently frozen just a few inches or centimeters below the surface. If a house is placed directly on the permafrost, its warmth melts the frozen ground, causing the house to settle unevenly into a wet, muddy hole. Houses are, therefore, built on stilts.

Life changes during the summer. From May through August, when the sun is above the horizon almost twenty-four hours a day, afternoons may see the thermometer climb to 70° F (+21° C) or higher.

Transportation and Communication in Barrow

Barrow, separated from the rest of the Arctic by the frozen Arctic Ocean to the north and from the rest of Alaska by the mighty Brooks Range mountains to the south, has no permanent road leaving for anywhere. In the winter there is a snow road that runs east along the coast to the Prudhoe Bay oil field more than 200 miles (322 km) away. Individuals do not drive on this road; only groups of trucks or huge tractors pulling sleds loaded with supplies do.

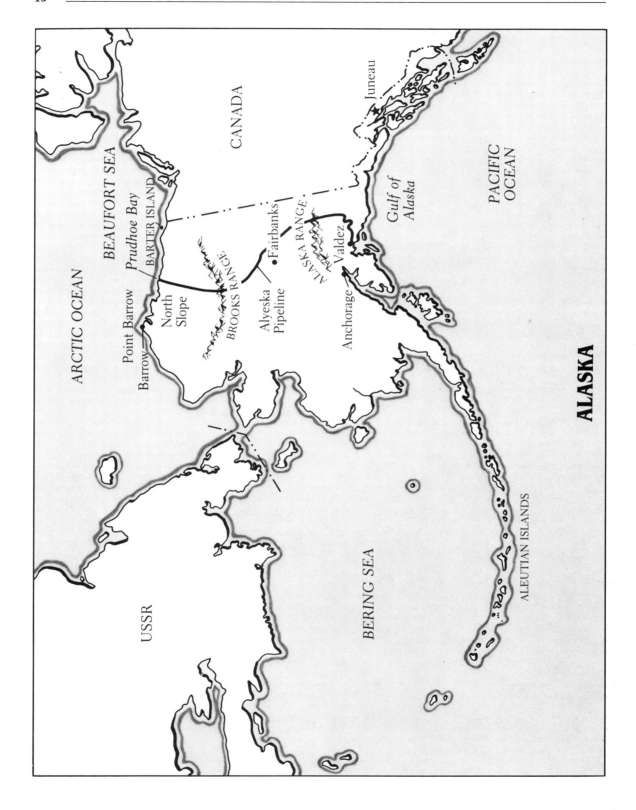

ALASKA

Permafrost affects roads and airports. Few roads are built because the repeated freezing and thawing cracks concrete or blacktop until it falls apart. The best roads in the Far North are those made by scrapping the permafrost smooth in the fall and letting it freeze solid in November. Ordinary trucks can drive on this frozen highway all winter long, for about eight months of every twelve. All truck traffic comes to a soggy stop by June, however, when the wheels churn the melting roadbed to mud. Only vehicles with treads (also called tracks), such as snowmobiles and bulldozers, can move through the mud. *Ecologists* want to forbid tracked vehicles going cross country in the summer because their tracks churn up the soil, melting the ground more deeply and permanently. This can destroy the fragile tundra plants and animals.

Snowmobiles were brought to Barrow to make transport over the snow easier than running behind a dog team. Snowmobiles became so popular that people began using them all year long because they could also carry people through the muds of summer. As soon as the snowmobile craze hit America and their cost went down, every Inuit and anyone else living in the North had to have one. Before long, many Inuit families in and around Barrow had two.

People get around town in Barrow in pickup trucks, taxis, cars, and also motorcycles. If absolutely necessary, people will walk. Only very rarely does someone drive a dog team into town. Most people have forgotten how to handle a dog team.

Although some expensive supplies may come to Barrow by plane, the town depends mainly on tall barges that come in during the short ice-free summer months. Occasionally, the ice is slow in breaking up, or a north wind keeps it close to shore, making the barges days or weeks late. The main subject of conversation in town is often about how late the barges are this year—and what might happen if they don't make it before a freeze.

To get any distance from Barrow, everyone flies. Almost every small village has an airstrip of some kind. Planes can land on the rivers and lakes with floats in the summer and skis in the winter. Two-engine propeller-driven planes take people from Barrow to more distant villages. Medium-size jets take people from Barrow to Fairbanks or Anchorage, where the giant jets stop on international trips from Europe over the North Pole to Asia.

Barrow has a telephone system for its three thousand people within the town, connecting them with many of the other villages and towns in Alaska. A new satellite in space now puts all of Barrow's telephone users in touch with the rest of the world. Villages without telephones usually have at least one shortwave radio that keeps them in contact with Barrow—when weather and atmospheric conditions will let the signals through.

Barrow also communicates by newspapers, most of which come in by plane from Fairbanks (*The Fairbanks Miner*), Anchorage (*The Anchorage Times*), and Seattle (*Seattle Sun*). *The New York*

The tundra in Alaska

Snowmobiles have largely replaced dogsleds as the means of transport in Barrow. Here a snowmobile is used to pull a sled.

The Inuit receive much of their food by plane or barge.

The post office at Barrow receives everything from groceries and medical supplies to postcards.

Times and *The Washington Post* arrive several days late. The Inuit also receive the *Tundra Times,* with local information of particular interest and importance for them.

In the 1980s the marvels of telecommunication came to Barrow and small villages and towns across northern Alaska. In a 1982 statewide contest, Alaska's schoolchildren named the new Satcom F-5 communication satellite "Aurora." Since then the adults have renamed it RATNET (Rural Alaska Television Network). All viewers, including the Inuit, are on committees that decide what programs will be shown to rural Alaskans. It's not surprising that what is most popular in the rest of America is what rural Alaskans also want to see.

Another system, the Learn/Alaska Network, brings educational programs to people from kindergarten through college age twenty-four hours a day. This new Low Power Television (LPTV) system is inexpensive enough that it can be set up even in small villages of thirty-five people. Two hundred sixty communities now have LPTV service.

The same satellite in space can also conduct an audio conference (no pictures) among many villages. Inuit people, for example, could have a conference to plan their future, with 160 towns talking together over the air.

Inuit Groups Communicate with Each Other

Inuit and other arctic peoples in Alaska, Canada, Greenland, Norway, and Siberia have similar backgrounds, interests, and problems, but are so far apart in distance that they'd never met as a group until 1977. That year they got together in Barrow for a modern version of a fair—the Inuit Circumpolar Conference.

The five-day conference was so successful that it's now being repeated every other year. One has since been held at Frobisher Bay, Baffin Island, Canada, just across from Greenland. Inuit came from all circumpolar nations except the Soviet Union. An empty chair was kept at the conference table to remind everyone that thousands of brothers and sisters in Siberia were not allowed to come. The conference studied such problems as the testing of cruise missiles in the Canadian subarctic, the location of MX missiles in Alaska, the use of atomic power plants in northern Canada, and the shipment of gas by ship from the newly discovered gas fields in Canada's arctic islands. The next conference is scheduled for Kotzebue, Alaska.

New Money Is Transforming Barrow

None of the changes in Barrow would have been possible before the oil discovery at Prudhoe Bay in 1969.

Barrow village is home for the North Slope Borough, which runs along the entire arctic coast from the Pacific Ocean side to the Canadian border, including Barrow and Prudhoe Bay with its oil and gas fields. Property taxes paid to the borough by Prudhoe Bay's oil companies make this the wealthiest municipality in the world. There are seven thousand citizens in the borough, and four thousand of them are Inuit. The Prudhoe taxes amount to $35,000 for each citizen each and every year. Individuals do not receive this money. Instead, it goes for services to improve their towns, villages, and schools.

The main town at Barrow intends to improve its quality of life by building water and sewage systems to serve every home and building. The town's yearly operating budget amounts to $200 million for only seven thousand citizens. Anchorage, an Alaskan city of 190,000 citizens, manages to operate with a budget of about the same amount. Part of this difference can be accounted for by the high cost of building, or of doing anything, in the Far North. For example, keeping water pipes from freezing in the frozen ground and, at the same time, keeping the warm sewage from melting the ground makes construction difficult and expensive. A system of water pipes will cost about $100,000 per man, woman, and child in Barrow.

In the past, the people have had to get fresh water either from the melt water on top of the frozen ocean, or, more recently, by tanker truck from a lake outside of town. Because the ground is frozen for most of the year, materials from all of the sinks and toilets in Barrow are frozen in barrels or plastic garbage bags and left out in the yard. The hope every year is that the truck will come to haul it out onto the ice pack offshore before the spring thaw comes. When the ice breaks up in summer, the bags and barrels float away on their little ice rafts and sink into the sea when the rafts finally melt. It's no wonder that water and sewer lines were of high priority when the oil money began flowing from Prudhoe.

The Alaska Native Claims Settlement Act

The Alaska Native Claims Settlement Act also has helped transform Barrow. For years Alaska's Inuit and Indians claimed that much of the land being selected as the new state of Alaska belonged to them. These groups argued that they had been there long before the white people arrived, and that the land's ownership had never been legally transferred from them to the U.S. government. Therefore, they said, the U.S. Congress had no right to give the land away to create a new state. In 1959 Alaska became the nation's forty-ninth state.

The natives of Alaska continued to press their case until 1971, when the Native Claims Settlement Act was passed. The act allowed Alaska's eighty-five thousand natives to keep 44 million acres (18 million hectares) of land, which is 12 percent of Alaska's land total. In addition, the U.S. government paid $1 billion for the rest of the land that the natives had lost to statehood. Thirteen regional corporations and two hundred village corporations were set up by the natives to receive and use this money to better their lives.

The Arctic Slope Regional Corporation in Barrow is one such example. These profit-oriented corporations can own hotels, oil fields, timberlands, reindeer herds, fisheries, fishing fleets, or anything that can yield profit for the stock-holding natives. Because there has not yet been much money made, some people fear that in 1996, when stockholders can sell their shares to oil companies, they will give away control over their remaining lands.

An Inuit Family in Barrow

Thanks to their high wages from the oil drilling, Joe Nageak and his wife, Faye, have recently moved from a small make-shift hut in Barrow to a larger frame house on metal stilts. The house is raised in this way so that the permafrost below doesn't melt. The house is oil-heated and warm even in Barrow's winter temperatures.

During the previous few years wages have risen so high, families have bought many modern conveniences by mail catalog. When the heavily loaded barges arrive from Seattle, Washington, in the summer, there's tremendous excitement. So many bright, modern, useful objects arrive: a new sofa, a color television, a stereo set, a microcomputer, and dozens of records and cassettes to enjoy during the year that will pass before the barges return.

Many of these new and valuable possessions must be thrown away when they break, since there are no computer or television repair stores in Barrow. Garbage disposal in Barrow is difficult because of the permafrost and ice, so each house looks like a magnet that has attracted metal to itself. Broken snowmobiles, trucks, motorcycles, refrigerators, and stoves surround the houses. Because of the dry, cold air, metal does not rust quickly, so these items may sit for years, joined by newer generations of broken equipment. With the newfound oil wealth of Barrow's residents and the complete lack of repair stores that other Americans take for granted, people in these small northern towns must buy new snowmobiles and refrigerators to replace the ones that break down.

With Joe at home, the Nageak family sits down to a meal of tea, canned fruit, potatoes, milk, and beer, with the center-piece a big caribou steak from last year's hunting. Except for the steak, which is a traditional Inuit food, the other goods are flown or barged in at great expense from the rest of the United States, almost 2,000 miles (3,220 km) to the south. These imported foods are very expensive. Today, with most Inuit living in towns and working for a salary, most traditional sources for food have been abandoned.

Joe and Faye Nageak remember a very different way of life before the oil was discovered in Alaska. They tell their children that not very long ago everyone had sled dogs, not snowmobiles; that people ate whale and fish, not bread and eggs; that winter coats were made from seal fur, not polyester; and that the long winter night was spent in repairing equipment and telling stories, not in watching television and going to basketball games.

At School in Barrow

Andy and Grace Nageak attend an ultra-modern public high school that opened in the winter of 1984–85. Barrow's school used to be run by the federal government's Bureau of Indian Affairs (BIA), and the only school had eight grades. Since all American students are required to go to high school, it meant flying to a BIA-approved school as far away as southern Alaska, Oregon, or even to an Indian school in Oklahoma. A new junior-senior high school was the first thing the people wanted, even before the water and sewer systems, and they wanted the best school that could be had. They now have for

Inuit children in Barrow play
a game called jumpboard.

*Barrow High School has taken years
to complete because of the difficulty
of building in the polar environment.*

their 275 native and white children a school with carpeted floors, television production studio, and heated swimming pool. At $71 million, Barrow's school cost perhaps ten times more than the cost of building a similar school in one of the other forty-nine states.

The Inuit have always been fond of sports and games, so the new school has the best sports program that money can buy. Basketball, the favorite sport, lures Barrow's players and fans to travel to Hawaii, more than 3,000 miles (4,830 km) away. That would be like a school in Boston playing an away game in Los Angeles.

The school board voted to pay the team's way and also decided to pay for the cheerleaders and a number of students to go. Another difficulty of being so far away from your competition is that no one can afford to come to Barrow for a home game. The school district has to pay for the outside team to fly up to Barrow.

In the past, very few Barrow Inuit ever went on to college. This was partly because of the high costs and partly because people could see no use for higher education. Now, however, the native-owned Arctic Slope Regional Corporation will send any qualified Barrow student "outside" to attend college, all expenses paid. The natives hope that highly trained and educated Inuit men and women will return with their law, engineering, and other degrees to help run the borough government and the native regional corporations for the betterment of their people. Some Inuit have already become members of the Alaska state legislature at the capital in Juneau, helping to keep that body aware of the needs of natives throughout the state.

A HISTORY OF
BARROW
AND ITS PEOPLE

The People

The Inuit, which the Eskimo prefer as their name (Eskimo means "eater of raw meat," an insulting name invented by an unfriendly Indian tribe), have lived at the top of the world for up to two thousand years (some areas have been inhabited longer than others).

Where did the Inuit come from? It is believed that at the end of the last Ice Age (about fifteen thousand years ago), sea levels were lower because a great deal of seawater was frozen into the great Ice Age glaciers that covered most of the continents. If you look at the map of Alaska, you can see the chain of Aleutian Islands that stretches toward the Soviet Union. When the sea level was lower, these islands formed a land bridge from Asia to North America. Experts believe it was this bridge that peoples of Asia crossed.

Most of these people moved south and east, to become the American Indian tribes. Some of them stayed, comfortable with the frozen world of the North, and became the Inuit tribes, moving eastward across what is now Canada and to Greenland.

Food, Travel, and Trade:
Traditional Ways

The waters off the northern coast of Alaska are home to many mammals and other marine life, which has made the area attractive to the Inuit. The bowhead whale is 45 to 60 feet (14 to 18 meters) in length; the beluga or white whale is much smaller (about 15 feet long, or 450 cm). Pods of walrus are also found on the ice, but the most numerous animals are the ringed, harbor, and bearded seals. These animals have long been basic to the Inuit way of life for food, clothing, tools, and many other valuable materials. Fish also have been important, especially during the summer. The main species caught include whitefish, tomcod, salmon, trout, and grayling.

Although many edible plants grow during the summer months, the Inuit of the coast did not use them for food because they were so geared to the sea and its produce. The Inuit of the Brooks Range ate many plants and were able to interest the coast dwellers in their berries, which they traded for ocean products such as seal oil and furs.

The Inuit of the Barrow area were involved in an elaborate trading system that went on year-round. Through this trading, they obtained even English and Russian goods years before they actually met any white people. All travel during the winter months was by dogsled, along

Inuit women wearing new parkas

the frozen rivers and lakes. During the short summer, some of the rivers were navigable, and at the ocean's edge there was room between the pack ice and the shore for the use of small skin boats called *umiaks*. The ice was very dangerous because it could always move in to shore. All longshore travel was done with great speed and caution.

Every spring Inuit from the mountains brought items to Point Barrow, some of which they had obtained from Siberians, who in turn had obtained things from the Russians. Point Barrow residents wanted the iron and copper kettles, double-edged knives, tobacco, beads, and tin that came from faraway Russia. In addition, the inland Inuit had themselves produced deer and fox furs and skins, feathers for headdresses and masks, and arrows. Barrow residents had their own products to trade with: whale and seal oil (for use as both food and fuel), whalebone, walrus tusks, sealskins, and so on.

Later in the summer, the Barrow Inuit would travel east to Barter Island, where they traded these items with Canadian Inuit and Indians. These natives had such products to offer as whale skins and stone lamps. In addition, they had obtained English trade goods from the great trading and exploration group, the Hudson's Bay Company. These valued items included knives, beads, guns, and ammunition. Far from being isolated and alone on their frozen coast, the Barrow Inuit were involved in a complicated flow of trade goods and learned quite a bit about Europeans before meeting any of them.

Early Inuit Homes

During the winter months, the Inuit lived in their villages, spending much time visiting each others' homes. Houses were scattered along permanent paths and looked like low mounds. That is because they were half-buried in the ground to keep them out of the cold winds. In order to dig the giant 5-foot (150-cm) deep hole for a house, the Inuit had to work during the hottest days of summer, when the sun would melt the permafrost enough for them to hack their way into the frozen ground. The end result was not unlike the ice-igloo (used by northern Canadian Inuit) in shape—a long entryway passage with many alcoves leading to a large round room with a domed roof. The big room served as sleeping quarters for the men and older family members. Inuit women

A house made of blocks of sod. In winter, the Inuit would pack snow over the structure. A hole at the top lets the smoke out.

lived and worked in the passageway, where they prepared food and stored cooking equipment, furs, and blankets.

The building materials included whale jaw bones for walls and archways, whale skulls for stepping-stones, driftwood for walls and floor planking, and sod to cover it all over. Even the coldness of the surrounding ground was made use of in the form of natural "deep freezes" for meat.

This kind of home was not the coast Inuits' only form of shelter. During the summer months, many Inuit families and friends would travel by boat to places for good fishing and hunting. They lived there for several weeks in shelters made of brush or tents made of furs and skins. These summer camps were often also the places where much of the trading with other groups took place. Summer was a festive, easy time, primarily because the sun never went down. People ate when hungry and slept when tired.

The Yearly Calendar of Activities

From April through June, the men of the villages of North Alaska organized themselves into hunting bands and camped on the edge of the sea ice, waiting with their tiny boats and bone harpoons to catch the giant bowhead whales. When one of these giants was killed, up to fifty tons of blubber and meat was divided among relatives and friends and stored in the big meat cellars around the village. Seals, ducks, and ptarmigan birds also were caught during this period.

In June, the time when the sea ice moves away from the shore, boats could go out to the drifting ice after walrus and seals. During June and July, other food sources included duck, caribou, and fish. In September, the ice pack moves back in to shore, and the rivers begin to freeze. At this time, the Inuit would prepare for winter by collecting fuel: driftwood from the beaches and coal from local coal veins. Ice was collected and stored in the cellar holes to be melted in winter for cooking and drinking.

As the sun vanishes in November, winter enters in full strength, and the Inuit then relied for food mostly on what they had stored during the warmer months. February brings hints of the end of winter, and soon the round of spring activities would begin again.

In addition to this yearly round of activities, the Inuit held two major festivals and many smaller ones each year. The first big one required that two villages pool their resources in December to hold a series of feasts, ceremonies, and gift-trading events. The other festival was held at the end of the whaling season to celebrate the year's catch.

Communication and the Arts

Inuit people from Alaska to Greenland understood—and still understand today—a common spoken language, although their accents might confuse one another from time to time, just as a Texan might have trouble understanding a person with a New York City accent.

The native peoples throughout the circumpolar region had no written language before the white people arrived. All of their stories, histories, religious

*Tents of a whaling camp. Women
and children participate in the camp,
but do not join the men in hunting.*

thoughts, and communications were oral. In the summer, the trading centers were communication spots. People would pick up new ideas and news about distant places and then inform their home villages.

Storytellers were important people. In a land where families might have to stay in their houses for days at a time while a blizzard raged outside, storytelling became an art. Inuit people used mime to tell much of the story, wore beautiful masks to represent animals and spirits, shook giant tambourines, and sang.

Most young people today don't understand the dancing and miming because the stories have to do with facing the tremendous force of nature, and they haven't had those experiences. A few people remember the old stories and dances handed down to them from their parents, but the art is in danger of dying out as the Inuit become more like the white people who have brought so many changes to their lands and minds.

When Christian missionaries came to stay with the Inuit, they realized that if people were to read the Bible or learn about other parts of the world, they'd have to have a written language. The Inuit language was then written down, and many of the white people's teachings were printed for the Inuit to read in their own tongue.

Art and Spiritual Belief

Because there was no early written language, Inuit peoples had expressed some of their thoughts through carving and sculpture. They carved wood or sculpted bone, ivory, and stone, depending on what materials were available locally or through trade. During the long winter night and the relaxed summer day, there was spare time to carve and sculpt many objects.

These carved objects often had a practical purpose. For example, a piece of whale tooth ivory might serve as the handle for a skinning knife. The ivory handle might be carved to look like a fox. Outsiders might think that this was simply decorative, but it had a more practical purpose in the mind of the carver. According to Inuit belief, because the piece of ivory now looked like a fox, the spirit of the next fox skinned with the knife would be happy and would allow the hunter to skin it more easily. Just having such a carved skinning knife on his belt would help an Inuit hunter to find a fox. Many of the Inuit carvings were done for such communication between people and the spirits of animals.

Good carvings also kept diseases away from a person or even from an entire village. Because death was always present in this difficult and dangerous environment, many of the Inuit carvings had to do with death. Some of the tiny ivory and stone carvings dug up today by *archaeologists* and *anthropologists* had been placed with bodies at burial. The Inuit believed that tiny models of useful objects like knives, lamps, harpoons, and kayaks placed in the grave would help a person in the next world. Missionaries have largely forced the Inuit to abandon the ideas of spirits being everywhere, so present-day carvings do not deal with the next life as much as with this one.

In the past, Inuit children had no toys other than what their parents carved out of wood, ivory, bone, or stone. Tiny

In the past, Inuit children used to play with carved toys like these dolls.

toys and games made of these materials helped children prepare themselves for the world of work and the difficult survival they'd soon meet.

The Outside World Arrives in Barrow

On a mission to map the Far North, the British ship HMS *Blossom* arrived off Point Barrow in 1826. Captain Beechey and his men visited the village. Other ships visited during the 1840s and 1850s, often wintering in the pack ice and trading with the Inuit. The first whaling ships appeared in 1854. In 1867 Alaska was purchased by the United States from Russia. By this time, dozens of whaling ships were

making the long coastal trip north from San Francisco—4,000 miles (6,400 km) one way—to catch the migrating bowhead, white, and other whales.

These sea mammals were used very differently by the Americans than by the Inuit. For one thing, meat and oil were not of as great value to the Americans as they were to the Inuit. The big whaling ships were after the whale's *baleen*. Instead of teeth, the whale has hundreds of long thin strips of baleen at the front of its mouth through which it filters tons of seawater to obtain its small particles of food.

Baleen is made of *keratin*, a flexible substance much like one's fingernails. It

An Inuit family butchers a whale

was in great demand in the United States and Europe, to be made into buttons and corset stays. (Corsets were nineteenth-century girdles worn by men and women to hold their stomachs in, and stays were the "ribs" that kept the corset stiff.)

Northern Alaska had continual coastal traffic of these big whaling ships until commercial whaling ground to a halt in the early twentieth century. The whalers were forced out of business by declining whale numbers and the development of substitute materials.

During the height of the commercial whaling, however, many Inuit and Indians from all along the coast and inland began to move to the main whaling centers. And their traditional patterns began to change as a result. No longer did they need to trade with their Indian and Inuit neighbors, because the whalers brought all sorts of goods right to the village: repeating rifles, ammunition, alcohol, flour, black tobacco, matches, lead, and molasses.

In return, the whalers wanted fresh water, whalebone, caribou meat, fur clothing, and souvenirs. They were eager for the Inuit carvings and sculpture, and they learned the art of carving, which they called scrimshaw, to while away the long ocean voyages. Over the years, many whalers set up formal and informal marriages with Inuit women, and a new community of families was established.

Soon there were more and more families living at Barrow—too many for a hunting society. Carving ivory became a new way of life for some of the more talented people. They began to earn money to buy "the good things of life."

The Inuit never objected to all the whaling. It didn't occur to them that all their whales could be killed by the white men, whom they saw at first as miraculous beings, with their harpoon guns and harpoons that exploded inside the whale.

Negative Effects of a New Life

There were serious and negative side effects to this new way of life, and these were obvious early on. The Inuit had no immunity to American and European diseases, for instance. Whole villages were wiped out by influenza, smallpox, and measles. In 1900 two hundred members of a group of inland Inuit, visiting Barrow to trade with the whalers, died after the ship departed. In 1902 more than one hundred Barrow Inuit died of the measles.

In addition to disease, alcohol brought great unhappiness. The Inuit were so fond of whiskey that they would trade large numbers of valuable furs for just one bottle. Alcoholism was and still remains a serious problem in these small, close-knit Inuit communities.

Another problem arose when Christian missionary groups and the Bureau of Indian Affairs arrived to set up schools for Inuit children. The aim of these schools was to produce Christians and United States citizens. It was hoped that the Inuit would give up what white society regarded as their "primitive" ways and become "modern."

The children often were separated from their parents for long periods and sent to distant locations for schooling. Many of these children failed to learn any of the traditional ways of getting food and living in the Arctic. At the same time, there were few local opportunities for them to get ahead as Christian Americans. Many social problems developed among the Inuit as a result of this educational policy.

Just as traditional Inuit trading practices came to an end, so many traditional food-gathering methods were soon abandoned. Families who did not want to be separated from their school-age children settled permanently in the villages where their children were in school. Soon the families forgot about going out in the summer for long periods to fish and hunt. Fathers worked for the whalers and traders for cash whenever possible, so they could buy more trade goods and attractive imported foods. Old skills were forgotten. A new way of life was taking over.

Bad Times
for Barrow
From the end of the whaling era in 1915 to the late 1940s following World War II, the Inuit were an unhappy and unhealthy people. They did not want to return to their former ways after getting used to American foods and goods, but there was no way for them to earn the cash they needed to buy these things. Their traditional community spirit and cooperation had disappeared.

The Inuit were encouraged by the United States government to try reindeer herding. Reindeer were imported from Siberia to replace the depleted caribou herds. This venture did not last, however. Other sources of income disappeared as well. The small amount of cash coming in

from fur-trapping vanished during the Great Depression of the 1930s.

At that time, when the entire Western world was caught in economic turmoil, the Inuit were forced by necessity to go back to some of their older ways of getting food. Because of this, some community spirit was revived. Also, new sources of cash began to arrive from the United States government: old age pensions and unemployment payments. There were also a few jobs available in post offices and government buildings and stores.

Carving as a
Source of Income
The government encouraged the Inuit to turn more to their art forms of carving and sculpture as a way of bringing in cash. It was hoped that the Inuit would set up a carving industry that would turn out pieces of traditional art in great quantities. The carving industry might then help solve the natives' economic plight. Such an approach, however, led to several problems.

The basic one was that art of any kind cannot be turned out rapidly, like automobiles. Artists do not and cannot work like that. Inuit carvers in particular could not work this way.

Another serious problem resulted when the white people selling the art found that people in New York, Montreal, or Paris loved the Inuit work but wanted larger pieces. The Inuit carvers had always worked with small pieces because of weight and scarcity of materials. Today they do carve larger pieces and also have begun to work in more modern styles, turning away from traditional designs.

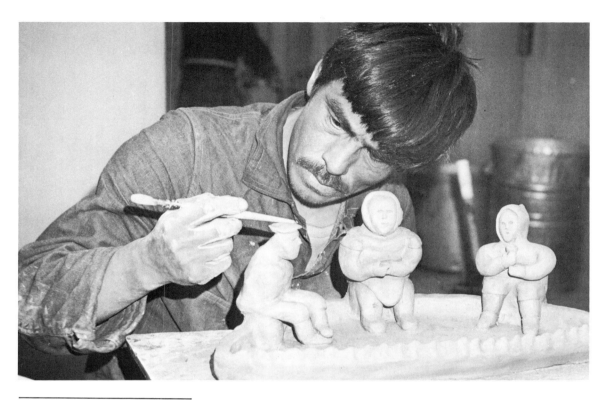

An Inuit craftsman at work

Unfortunately, when a whole village works at turning out pieces of art for sale, there will be a few exceptional pieces and many that are not very good. Today a traveler can buy pieces of this mass-produced artwork at airports around the world. This is good for the Inuit because it brings in cash. But will these mass-production artists still have pride in their ancient culture's art forms? Or will they see it as merely a way of earning money?

Recent Years in Barrow and the Discovery of Oil

Geologists had known for many years that great amounts of oil and gas probably lay below Barrow and all along the Arctic coast. In 1946 the U.S. Navy set up its Arctic Research Laboratory and began prospecting for oil. A big camp was built near Barrow, and the Inuit were encouraged to find jobs there as janitors, cleaning women, and guides for geology crews. The government also began to map the region in greater detail, and other government agencies and missionary efforts provided more jobs. Since World War II, Barrow has been a small but important U.S. government center in the frozen North.

From 1953 to 1957, another source of work for Inuit men was as members of the

A section of the Alyeska pipeline

construction crews building the Distant Early Warning (DEW) radar installations all along the north coast. This equipment is designed to give the first warning if the Soviet Union sends aircraft or atomic missiles across the North Pole to attack Canada and the United States.

Change came to the Inuit even faster in 1969, when oil was discovered at Prudhoe Bay, 200 miles (322 km) east of Barrow. That date may mark for historians the time when the Inuit culture quickly became lost and the Inuit people became more like all other American citizens.

Prudhoe Bay has been spouting gas, oil, and dollars ever since the Alyeska pipeline began to operate in 1978. This giant pipe (more than 6 feet, or 1.8 meters, in diameter) begins at Prudhoe Bay on the Arctic Ocean's shore, runs through the Brooks Range, across the tundra and *muskeg* to Fairbanks, and then all the way south to the ice-free port of Valdez on the Gulf of Alaska, a total distance of about 750 miles (1,208 km). Oil tankers then carry the oil to the west coast of the lower United States for final refining. The pipeline's greatest capacity is 2 million barrels of oil per day.

The oil fields needed laborers and paid unusually well. Because Inuit men could work better than most white men in the severe weather, they were hired as soon as they walked into the oil company's offices asking for work.

Even before the Prudhoe Bay oil discovery, men had been going "outside" to earn money in major Alaskan cities like Fairbanks and Anchorage. When the men returned to Barrow, they impressed their families and friends with some of the objects they'd brought home from the cities —refrigerators, stoves, stereo record players, radios, and, later on, television.

Television certainly affected everyone in America, but not as dramatically as it did the Inuit in the Far North. Now they could see for themselves just how their fellow citizens lived in the other states. By contrast, they could also see how little they had and what uncomfortable lives they led. The more the men, women, and children saw on television, the more they wanted. The more they wanted, the more dollars they needed. The only jobs available in the bigger cities at that time were for men, so Inuit families had to stay at home, husbandless and fatherless—something totally new for the Inuit.

Current Problems

While working in the larger towns and cities, far away from their families, many of the men spent their evenings drinking with other lonely men. Then they began to take liquor back to their homes to drink during the rest of the year. Alcohol has caused so many problems within Inuit and white families in the Far North that more than fifty native villages and towns have recently voted to outlaw the sale of liquor in their areas. If the men drink too heavily, as some do, they can't give much guidance or attention to their sons and daughters. Family violence, one result of too much drinking, has increased greatly. Most native leaders say that alcoholism is the greatest problem the Inuits have.

Community Spirit

Even with all the problems brought by change, it is still true that the Inuit are a strong and hopeful people. Barrow's community enthusiastically supports a wide range of civic groups, and religion is very important to the residents. There are many clubs and activities and a bustling social life among people of all ages.

Today the Inuit celebrate American holidays, although they do retain the whale season festival in early summer. Thanksgiving may include a church feast, group singing, drumming, and dancing. Between Christmas and New Year's there is a continual round of feasts, games, church services, and dogsled and snowmobile races.

RESOURCE USE AND THE FUTURE

Just as the ancient Inuit used to consider their carvings and other works of arts and crafts as a way to communicate with and fight off evil spirits, they thought of their natural resources simply as materials by which to survive in a harsh and dangerous environment. There were so few Inuit in the old villages and fishing camps that they couldn't ruin the environment or use up any resource. They didn't mine minerals beyond the open coal seams. They made great use of rocks and driftwood. They

An Inuit graveyard with a fence of whale-back bones and Christian crosses

didn't grow vegetables, grains, or fruits. Most Inuit lived north of the forests, so they didn't make much use of timber.

Before the white men came, the Inuit lived in such small groups that it seemed the environment and its natural resources were limitless. And for such small groups, they were. Considering the amount of usable meat from a whale (up to 100,000 pounds, or 45,000 kg), it would take only one large whale to feed a village over the winter. Even the small, more easily caught beluga whale would supply its hunters with more than 1,000 pounds (450 kg) of meat. Because thousands of whales were born every year, the Inuit didn't have to worry about running out of whale. They might have a bad year and not catch a single one, but they knew there would be more the next year, and substitutes were available—a walrus carcass also could supply a small village with enough food and fuel for a long period.

As recently as forty years ago, when only about thirty families lived in Barrow, everyone lived almost entirely on food obtained from the sea. Once in a while they had caribou and smaller land animals. These animals are no longer a resource because the Inuit no longer have the time to hunt them. Whales and seals might be abundant, but if no one remembers how to use them, they are no longer resources. The young people of today also prefer American foods such as hamburgers and fries.

Thirty years ago the Inuit did not think of oil and gas as valuable resources. Now, however, they realize that oil and gas have helped make them prosperous.

By the time the oil and gas run out,

sometime in the not too distant future, the Inuit will not know how to survive as hunters, nor will they be happy living without money and all that it buys. Their lives have changed forever, and so have their ideas about what is a valuable natural resource.

What Other Resources Do the Inuit Have?

What other resources do the Inuit have to develop? Barrow has money resources today, but this comes almost entirely from taxes on Prudhoe's oil and gas production. When that dries up, the North Slope Borough may still have money in the bank, but it could probably not attract many industries and people to move to the Far North.

The climate and beauty of a place can be regarded as resources if they attract tourists, the wealthy, and retired people who bring money to spend. Barrow certainly has a distinctive climate and setting, but because they won't attract people in great numbers, they cannot be called resources.

Fertile soils are excellent natural resources, but the severe cold of the Far North prevents good soil from developing. There can be no agriculture around Barrow except in greenhouses with soils brought in from elsewhere. When the oil and gas give out, the Inuit cannot turn to farming even if they want to. They could become reindeer herders, selling reindeer milk, meat, and skins to earn a post-oil living. Or they might raise musk oxen for their excellent warm wool and high-protein meat. Whales, walruses, and seals could be harvested for their meat, oil, and other products; and arctic fox, ermine, and polar bears could be harvested for their meat and furs. But many Inuit may not want to live this outdoor life again.

What Is the Future For
Oil and Gas Production?

More oil and gas reserves have been located north of Alaska in the Beaufort Sea. A number of artificial islands were built in that shallow sea for drill platforms on which drilling crews live and work. The destructive power of the ice pack as it moves with the sea currents and the winds makes construction and work extremely difficult, however. Some of the Inuit who worked on the drilling rigs at Prudhoe Bay found new work on these exploratory wells. When these wells begin producing, the transfer of oil and gas to the pipelines at Prudhoe Bay will create problems for the owners and work for the workers. Some of the exploratory wells in the Beaufort Sea are partly native-owned corporations, so their success is doubly important for the Inuit.

Perhaps many years from now the coal resources under the lands owned by the Barrow Inuit will become profitable to operate. Now that people have learned how to build pipelines in permafrost regions, there may be a way to move coal through pipelines as a partly liquid slurry, as is now done in other coal-mining states. The Inuit cannot depend wholly on this resource because so much of the coal in the world is much more easily mined and transported. But perhaps it is a future resource. Other minerals are mined elsewhere in Alaska, but not many have been found within the North Slope Borough's lands.

The region's economic development will always be difficult because of various stresses. Some stresses come from the natural environment itself; others come from technologies brought in from the south. Technologies that may have worked well in the environment where they were developed do not do as well with the unique stresses put on them in the Arctic cold.

Final Thoughts About
the Future of the Inuit

Many questions remain about the Inuit and their changing way of life. Must they give up their old ways? Should the whites dictate how an environment should be thought of and acted on? This is almost the same question that arises about the Inuit and their sculpture. Should they be forced by economics to carve differently than people have for thousands of years? The answers are not obvious, and they will be discussed for many years to come.

3

CHERSKIY, IN THE SOVIET UNION

It is a day in early winter, and the October light will soon fade from the sky. After school, Olga is visiting Yelena, who lives with her parents and brother in a five-story, gleaming-white apartment house. Next to it, in an orderly row, are four more identical white boxes, set on the edge of the growing Siberian Arctic town of Cherskiy. When Yelena looks out of the front window, she sees the other apartment houses and beyond them the lights of town. If she walks into the bedroom and looks out of the back window, she sees land empty of humans. Scraggly pine trees and bogs march off to the south.

Cherskiy sits on a high piece of land that juts out into the majestic Kolyma River. By the time the river gets to the town of Green Cape (Zelenyy Mays is its Russian name) 4 miles (6.4 km) to the north, there are no trees at all, and the tundra stretches to the frozen shores of the Arctic Ocean. But south of Cherskiy begins the *taiga*, the great cold forest of larch, pine, and fir that covers much of the mountainous, river-cut regions of Siberia.

Yelena's father and mother, both engineers, moved to Cherskiy all the way from Moscow, the Soviet capital, 3,200 miles (5,210 km) away. At first they disliked the empty landscape. But the high wages, good housing, and availability of consumer goods—so scarce in Moscow—made them stay on.

Yelena was born in Cherskiy, and the great empty spaces do not trouble her. She sees the land as something to be developed for the betterment of her life, her parents' lives, and the lives of other citizens of the Soviet Union.

Yelena likes the view of open land from her apartment because that is where her friend Olga's family lives. Unlike Yelena's family, whose ancestors lived in European Russia to the west, Olga's ancestors have lived in the tundra and taiga for centuries. Her people herd reindeer and trap animals for food and fur. Olga's family belongs to an *ethnic* group, the Yakaghir, one of a dozen groups of native Siberians who live in the Soviet Arctic. There are an estimated three hundred thousand native Siberians, now citizens of the Soviet Union. As with the Inuit and Indians of Alaska, the Siberian natives are mostly settled in towns and encouraged to become modern Soviet citizens. Even though Olga's family lives for some of the time in Cherskiy and Olga attends school in town, her family is often far away, tending their herds. During these times, Olga visits them on vacations. In any northern settlement, the native Siberians are far outnumbered by the European settlers, who arrived over the past four hundred years.

Today Cherskiy is a rapidly growing center for mining, herding, and shipping. The history of the area suggests that, just as in Alaska, there have been good and bad times for the natives. For those settlers originally from western Russia, Siberia has been, over the past centuries, a place of freedom and a place of terror.

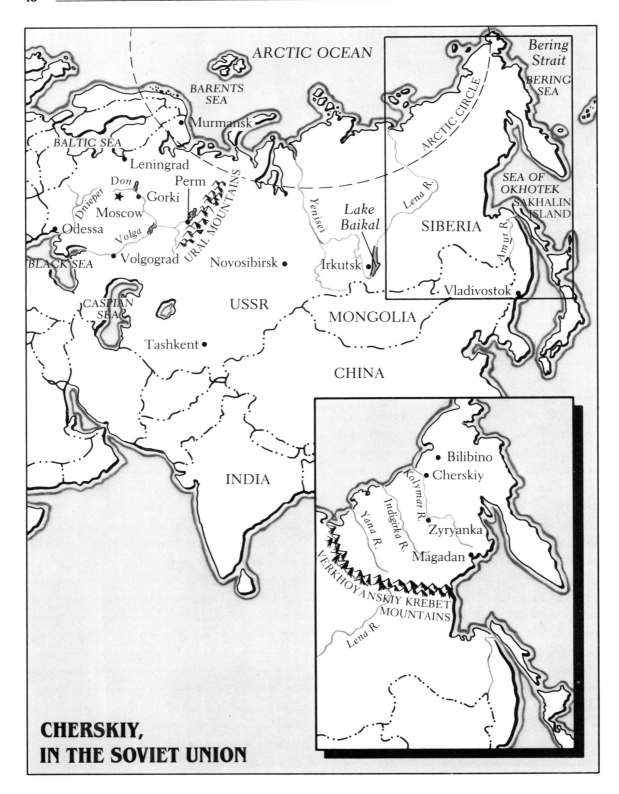

ARCTIC OCEAN

BARENTS SEA

Murmansk

BALTIC SEA

Leningrad

Don

Perm

Gorki

Dnieper

Moscow

Odessa

Volga

Volgograd

BLACK SEA

CASPIAN SEA

USSR

Tashkent

INDIA

Novosibirsk

URAL MOUNTAINS

Yenisei

Lake Baikal

Irkutsk

MONGOLIA

CHINA

Bering Strait

BERING SEA

ARCTIC CIRCLE

Lena R.

SIBERIA

SEA OF OKHOTEK

SAKHALIN ISLAND

Amur R.

Vladivostok

Bilibino

Cherskiy

Kolymar R.

Indigirka R.

Yana R.

Zyryanka

Magadan

VERKHOYANSKIY KREBET MOUNTAINS

Lena R.

CHERSKIY, IN THE SOVIET UNION

How can two such different descriptions be attached to one region?

THE PLACE

The Soviet Union, or Union of Soviet Socialist Republics (USSR), is almost 7,000 miles (11,200 km) from west to east, more than twice as wide as the United States, and 2,500 miles (4,000 km) from north to south. At 8,649,490 square miles (22,488,674 sq km), it is the largest country in the world. During the twentieth century, the Soviet Union has brought many nations and peoples together under one government. On its western borders, it is European in culture and climate. On its eastern and southern borders, it has many different peoples and a wide variety of climates. In the far northeast, from the Kolyma River east to the Bering Strait, the people and the land have much in common with Alaska.

Siberia is a huge part of the Soviet Union. At about 2.9 million square miles (7.5 million sq km), it extends east across northern Asia from the Ural Mountains to the Pacific Ocean. In the north, Siberia borders the Arctic Ocean. In the south, it reaches as far as China and Mongolia.

Half of Siberia is underlain by permafrost. Its northern third lies within the *Arctic Circle*. Central Siberia's temperatures can be both much colder than Alaska's, plunging down to minus 90° F (−68° C) in winter, and as high as 90° F above zero (32° C) in the brief summer. The area around Cherskiy on the Kolyma River is not as extreme, but it is still very cold. The Arctic Ocean north of Cherskiy is frozen ten months of the year. Only the South Pole has temperatures as continuously cold as in Siberia. Materials, machines, and people have to work at ninety below zero and ninety above zero. They all sometimes fail under such stress.

As in northern Alaska, precipitation is low. There is less than 10 inches (25 cm) of rain and snow a year in the area of Siberia that includes Cherskiy. Winter days are dry, still, and cold enough to kill unprotected people. April sees the rivers thaw, and soon the short warm summer arrives with its mosquitoes. By late August, night frosts and snow flurries return, and river ice develops by late September.

Tundra, Taiga, and Topography

The tundra stretches south from the Arctic Ocean to meet the taiga about 50 miles (80 km) from the mouth of the Kolyma River. The *tree line*, where the taiga begins, is not sharp and sudden. Instead, at its northern edge there is a broad band of land that supports a few trees, struggling to survive on the tundra. Some of these trees may be only 2 feet (60 cm) tall, but over a hundred years old. Farther south the number of trees gradually increases to forest density.

In summer the tundra supports vegetation familiar to northern Alaskans: mosses, lichens, sedge grasses, and willow shrubs. The taiga is a vast and seemingly endless forest cover, marching over the mountains and lowlands of Siberia. Much of it has never been cut. The main northern tree types are black spruce, pine, larch, and fir, which can survive the lack of water in the frozen soil. In the southern and western regions of Siberia, greater moisture and higher temperatures add oak, maple, ash, and birch to the list.

The *topography*, or shape of the land, varies across Siberia. In the south and west are vast flatlands, regions of lakes and bogs, and belts of fertile farmland. In the Soviet Far East, which is one official name for the Cherskiy region, the land is made up of rugged and impassable mountain ranges drained by several major rivers. These in-include the Olenk, Lena, Yana, Indigirka, and Kolyma. The major mountain masses are the Cherskiy, Kolyma, and Verkhoyan-ski Krebet.

THE PEOPLE AND HOW THEY USE THE LAND

Because of the vast distances and difficult environment and climate, for centuries Siberia was isolated from Russia, west of the Urals. This isolation enabled native peoples of Siberia to develop ways of living very different from those of Europe.

The isolation and emptiness also attracted European Russian settlers. They wanted to live free of the oppressive government of the *tsars*, who ruled the land then known as Russia up to 1917. The wealth of fur-bearing animals and rumors of gold and diamonds brought many explorers and adventurers into the region.

Isolation also made the region ideal for the creation of giant slave labor camps to imprison people who did not agree with the government. Finally, Siberia's isolation and bleakness prevented, until very recently, the discovery that it is a treasure trove of natural resources. Many new mineral deposits and oil and gas fields are still being identified and mapped.

The Native Peoples of the Soviet Far East

The ancient native inhabitants of the region around Cherskiy made use of both the tundra and taiga. Some of the groups were like North American Inuit, and others had more in common with the Lapps of northern Scandinavia.

As you remember from the section on Alaska, the original Inuit and Indians traveled across the Bering Strait from northeastern Siberia to Alaska. They accomplished this by skin boats in summer and dogsleds in winter. These ties were maintained through trading for centuries. In the 1950s, the Soviet government broke the chain by moving all Inuit from the Bering Strait islands to the USSR mainland.

The Yakaghir

In the Soviet Union today, there are about three hundred thousand native inhabitants. They live along the shores of the Arctic Ocean and south into the taiga. The Yakaghir, who have long lived along the Kolyma River, today number about eight hundred. Once they numbered in the thousands. For centuries they have hunted sea mammals in their ocean-front villages and herded reindeer inland. They have a legend about their past:

"There was a time when so many Yakaghir fires were burning that their smoke darkened the wings of birds trying to fly north in the spring. Moreover, the northern lights are nothing less than the reflection of numerous Yakaghir campfires left in the memory of the sky" (quoted in Yuri Rytkheu, "People of the Long Spring," *National Geographic* 163, no. 2 [1983]).

Today many of the Yakaghir are European-educated and trained, but most of them prefer to remain on the land in their traditional occupations. In contrast to the political ferment going on among the Alaskan natives, the Yakaghir and other natives of Siberia are not in a position to gain greater control over their future. The Soviet government, while understanding the Yakaghir's traditional way of life, is not sympathetic to calls for change. Communication is forbidden between the Siberians and other Arctic groups.

Settlement from the West

Centuries ago Siberia was largely unknown to Europeans and Russians. Ice-locked and silent, these vast lands were open to anyone willing to give up the comforts of the west. For many European settlers of this period, the more livable parts of Siberia were havens from political persecution.

The tsars ruled Russia then. The tsarist government had the power of life or death over its citizens. Even the wealthy landowners and aristocrats lived in fear of the tsar's secret police. Criminals and anyone who disagreed with the tsar's government were banished to a life of hard labor beyond the Urals.

But Siberia was a place of hope as well as punishment in those days. The majority of the Russian people were poor peasants who lived a back-breaking existence as farmers for the rich landowners. For them and others, Siberia promised deliverance and freedom, much as the Americas did for many millions of Europeans.

By 1700 there were an estimated two hundred thousand Russian settlers east of the Ural Mountains. Most of their villages and farms were on land less rugged than that found in the Soviet Far East. A settlement, Nizhniye Kresty, was built on the Kolyma River in 1644, at the site of today's Cherskiy. A *Cossack*, Semyon Dezhnev, built a tiny fort and traded for furs with the Yakaghir, Evenki, and Chukchi native groups.

By 1710 there were several settlements in the Kolyma River valley and along its *tributaries*. Many of these people were gold prospectors. In 1784 Russian exploration and settlement had moved to the North American mainland in Alaska, and several forts and towns were maintained there until the United States purchased Alaska in 1867.

In 1710 Tsar Peter the Great made Siberia an administrative province of Russia. Its capital was located at Tobolsk, just east of the Urals. This event changed the life of the natives of Siberia.

The tsar's government had found that Siberia was rich in minerals. Soon giant labor camps were set up to mine them. The labor camps were populated by political prisoners and criminals from all over Russia. Their families often accompanied them to Siberia. Many thousands died on the trip, and others died later due to the severe and cruel conditions under which they were forced to live and work.

The Kolyma Forced-Labor Region

In 1917 the tsar's government fell during the Russian Revolution. Several years of turmoil followed the revolution. During these years, a communist government was established in Russia. The new leaders changed the name of the country to the Union of Soviet Socialist Republics, or the USSR.

The Siberian exiles from the time of the tsars were released. But they were soon replaced by thousands of people who disagreed with the new government. The Soviet government set up camps of complete isolation in northwestern Siberia for enemies of the Soviet state and members of ethnic and racial groups regarded as untrustworthy.

When Josef Stalin led the Soviet Union—from the late 1920s to the early 1950s—the entire Kolyma River basin, from the Arctic Ocean on the north to the Sea of Okhotsk on the south, became a region of forced labor. In this thousand-mile area of terror, prisoners slaved, usually under inhuman conditions. They did the back-breaking work of natural resource development: tree felling, coal and gold mining, and construction. Housing was poor, food was a bad joke, and the future promised no improvement. Some sources estimate that about 15 to 16 million people died of exhaustion and starvation in the prisons and labor camps of Stalin's time.

The Soviet Government Adopts a Less Cruel Approach

Since the death of Stalin in 1953, this harsh approach to resource development has changed somewhat. Siberia is still a place of exile for thousands of *dissidents*, as those who disagree with the government are called today. Camps and isolated towns of exile continue to exist.

The government's purpose in sending political prisoners to Siberia is not so much to punish them as to keep them out of the major cities so that their ideas will not attract large audiences. Because a person must have official papers in order to get around in the USSR, it is difficult to impossible to escape by plane, boat, truck, or on foot. There are so few roads, railroads, and airports that the police would very soon find someone without proper travel papers, work permits, and personal identification. Political prisoners are still sent to Cherskiy, where they work for the development of the north.

The Soviet government is trying to attract settlers to the region by promising better conditions than what people have in western Russia. This has attracted many people like Yelena's parents to Siberia's new towns.

The Northern Sea Route Opens Siberia

Between 1920 and 1970 a shipping route was opened up along the northern coast of Siberia. This coast is ice-bound six or more months of the year. The Soviet government developed special icebreaker ships to plow through the pack ice, leaving an ice-free but temporary path for merchant ships following behind. The entire North Sea Route from Murmansk to Vladivostok is 6,600 miles (10,600 km) long.

Icebreakers have helped open up northern Siberia to development.

A new town in Siberia. These are apartment buildings.

This route has finally made it possible for the Soviet government to get at the resources of northern Siberia. There are still no railways or roads, so shipping and air flight are the only methods for moving raw materials and finished goods to places where people can use them. A northern Trans-Siberian railroad is in the early stages of planning and construction.

The new towns of Siberia have been built to house the workers and to create permanent settlements in an almost empty part of the world. Industrial plants are being built in these towns also. The plants process the natural resources, refine them, and make them into finished products

right in Siberia. The government believes that this approach is better than transporting tons of raw materials elsewhere for finishing. Most important, the Soviet government is certain that the future of the nation depends on the development of Siberia.

CHERSKIY TODAY: AN ADMINISTRATION AND TRANSPORTATION CENTER

Cherskiy serves as the administration capital and transportation center for the Kolyma region. Because large ships can't get quite this far up the Kolyma River, they load and unload at Green Cape, 4 miles (6.4 km) north, near the river's mouth. During the summer, materials brought by the ships along the Northern Sea Route to Green Cape are moved south to Cherskiy and beyond on self-propelled river barges. During the winter, trucks (called boats) run on the solidly frozen Kolyma River, delivering supplies to camps in the huge gold fields to the south. The returning barges carry the gold and some coal from the surface mines near Zyryanka to be loaded on ships heading back to the western USSR. Some trucks will go as far as 700 miles (1,120 km) south on dirt roads to Magadan on the Pacific Coast, where the icebreakers keep the port open all winter.

Trucks also run east along the Arctic coast on roads built of frozen permafrost, as at Barrow, but the Soviets' transport system is more highly organized. Hundreds of trucks and a thousand drivers keep supplies going along this road all winter. Warm rest stops for drivers and repair shops for their trucks are set at 100-mile (160-km) intervals. Tracked rescue vehicles patrol the hundred-mile station-to-station links between Cherskiy and the atomic power station at Pevek, and into the gold fields at Bilibino.

Special Services for the People

The Polar Aviation Service provides services to those northern communities with a thousand or more people. It flies three to four thousand aircraft of all kinds along the edge of the Arctic Ocean, all the way from Murmansk near Norway to the Bering Strait near Alaska. Cherskiy has as many as one hundred thousand passengers passing through in one year. The Polar Aviation Service provides doctors, ambulances, mail, ice mapping for ships moving through the Northern Sea Route, and supplies for trappers and reindeer herders. In addition, all necessary services are delivered by air to scientists studying on the many ice islands floating in the Arctic Ocean. The Soviet government's attitude is that if people are to work in these strange and cold lands, they'd better be provided with convenient and comfortable air transport wherever they want to go.

Since every Soviet citizen has the right to free medical care, a large system of health services had to be established to serve the people of the Kolyma region, with the main hospital in Cherskiy. Doctors, nurses, and paramedics are always ready to jump into a helicopter and head out to some remote mining camp to provide emergency, or even routine, medical services.

Working with Permafrost

Permafrost, called merzlota in Russian, causes the same construction problems in Cherskiy that it does at Barrow. The Soviet engineers have an unusual method to make sure the buildings won't sag down into melted permafrost. When they want to sink concrete columns down into the permafrost to support buildings, they use steam jets to melt holes for the pre-formed columns to be dropped down into. Then they wait for the permafrost to refreeze solidly around the columns.

The permafrost that grips these supporting columns might still melt in the heat of summer if the engineers didn't do something else unusual—they eliminate the first floor of their arctic buildings, making them stand high on these stilts of concrete. By letting air flow freely across the shaded ground under the building and by keeping the warmth of the building high above the permafrost, this system ensures that the ground stays frozen around the supporting stilts even during the summer.

Siberians try to make nature work for them, whenever possible. For example, when they net huge numbers of salmon and other fish in the Kolyma River during the summer, they use the cold of the permafrost to preserve them. They dig a "mine" shaft about 60 feet (1,800 cm) down through the permanently frozen ground and then dig out radiating tunnels, as in a coal mine. The fish freeze completely just by being left in the tunnels. Endless conveyor belts move the heavy fish (some heavier than 50 pounds, or 22.5 kg) from the shaft out through the maze of branching tunnels. The fish are then taken from the river bank on a narrow-gauge railroad up to the central shaft. One such "mine" or "deep freeze locker" can store up to a million pounds of fish. Any fish not used locally or up the Kolyma River are sent by refrigerator ships from Green Cape west to Murmansk, Moscow, and other cities throughout the Soviet Union.

The New Settlers

Settlers from western parts of the Soviet Union still tend to return home after two or three years in Siberia. But the Soviet government does as much as possible to encourage the settlers to stay longer, or even permanently. For example, housing has improved. In the past, engineers in Cherskiy used to build log houses using the trees from the vast taiga forest. But now they build with concrete. One reason for the change had to do with the attitudes of the people.

New settlers thought of their jobs as exciting, different, and well paid, but temporary. Because log houses looked temporary, people tended to think of themselves as temporary residents, returning to their home areas after only a year or so. By switching from log houses to concrete apartment buildings that are similar to those in Moscow or other large cities in the south and west, people are now content to stay longer, even permanently.

Another way of keeping settlers is by offering higher wages than people get back home. As soon as a worker arrives in Cherskiy, his or her salary is set 40 percent higher than it was back home. This is increased another 10 percent every six months, so that by the time the worker has been there five years, his or her salary is much greater than what someone back home is earning for the same job. These "pioneers" are given cars, free travel, and extra vacations. The typical worker in Cherskiy receives almost two months of vacation per year, with free air travel anywhere within the Soviet Union. The pay and extras are so good that some people from Moscow go out to Siberia for a few months just to make some additional money.

Siberian settlers also avoid the severe shortage of housing in Moscow, where several families may have to share an apartment. Most people in Cherskiy have their own apartment with a bathroom.

People also like the excitement of working together to create something new—in this case, a town and a region. The challenge of living in such a harsh environment, although sometimes uncomfortable, makes life more interesting for some people.

The non-natives of Cherskiy living in their Moscow-like apartments like to have food that reminds them of home. Although food is brought in from all over the Soviet Union to keep people happy, local food is also consumed. Gradually, the inhabitants learn to like smoked horse colt's tongue, reindeer sausage, and horse milk. The local fish supply is excellent: several varieties of salmon, cod, and herring in unending supply. A favorite soup eaten throughout the Soviet Union is ukha, made differently by different cooks, but usually containing three or four different types of fish, potatoes, onions, peppers, and lots of salt.

At School

Olga and Yelena often work together on school projects. Olga thinks she would like to be a nutritionist or a doctor when she grows up, but everything will be decided in the next year when the two girls are in eighth grade.

All children in the Soviet Union must go to school, but their choices are limited by the system. At the eighth grade level, everyone takes tests to find out who will go on to what kind of further schooling. The student can follow the normal path and go through what Americans would call tenth grade. After that, only the very best students, or those whose parents have money or power, may go to the universities or some highly specialized institute.

Others may go to a *technikum*, or technical school, to become middle-level technicians and factory foremen. Still others may go to a vocational school to learn specific trades or skills. If a student's parents are high up in government or in the universities, the child may go to "special schools" from the first grade through the tenth. These elite schools produce the country's future leaders of science, industry, and government. They are not unlike prep schools in the United States. For inhabitants of Siberia, a university education and technical training mean spending several years far from home at a school in European Russia or southern Siberia. Educated and trained Siberians are expected to return to their homes to bring new skills to the giant task of taming the cold, empty spaces.

The Native Siberians Today: The Yakaghir

There are only two or three thousand native people living in or around Cherskiy. These are the Yakaghir, some Evenki, and a few Chukchi. Although some of these native people work their way up to positions in the local government, such as the mayor of Cherskiy, most of them prefer other work. Most Yakaghir, for example, would rather herd reindeer because their people have always done that kind of work. The Soviet government has encouraged the Yakaghir to continue to raise reindeer herds of great size. Some of the finest reindeer herds in Siberia are worked out of Cherskiy. Young men and women from the reindeer-herding families are sent to other parts of the country to study the latest methods of herding, slaughtering,

A Soviet schoolroom.
Opposite: A grocery
store in Siberia

*Reindeer herders talking
with a visiting doctor*

and transporting meats, skins, milk, and other reindeer products.

The reindeer herds all belong now to the state collective farm. A collective farm's land, equipment, and herds are owned by the state, which makes the decision regarding what will be produced. But each herder has a few of his own animals that he's allowed to run with the state-owned herds. The herders share in the profits of the collective. Reindeer meat is extremely high in protein, and the animals need little tending. Thus, raising reindeer is very profitable.

Yakaghir herders live in permanent villages. Helicopters are sometimes used to carry doctors, visitors, and supplies out to the tundra where other Yakaghiri have set up their big reindeer-skin tents, called *yarangas*. It is this group's turn to oversee the herd of three thousand reindeer.

The animals and tents are moved every two or three days as the frosty moss and lichens are consumed. Once a week a herder takes a team of reindeer south to the forest for a load of firewood. Supplies and mail are brought weekly by air to the *nomads*, who live both their ancient life of wandering and a modern town life.

Native Housing

The Yakaghiri tent homes are quite comfortable. Inside the double layer of skins is a room carpeted with soft robes made from reindeer fur. There is no furniture other than a small stove and table. In the other tents of the camp, the women cook and clean skins. The men and boys tend the herd.

Among the Yakaghir, certain jobs are for women, and others are for men. The Yakaghir have always divided the work this way. At school in Cherskiy, the children are taught that modern Soviet workers must learn a skill regardless of their gender, but the Soviet government is willing to support the Yakaghir and other native groups in keeping alive part of their past.

Although the herders continue the work of their ancestors, their lives have changed in some respects. For example, they have radios to call in a helicopter for emergencies or to call out the next group of herders while the first group is flown back to Cherskiy for several weeks of rest and relaxation.

RESOURCE USE: TODAY AND TOMORROW

According to a recent estimate, Siberia contains the bulk of the Soviet Union's natural resources: 75 percent of the nation's timber, 70 percent of its hydroelectric potential, 70 percent of its ores, 80 percent of its coal reserves, and probably its largest deposits of oil and gas.

Yet until recently Siberia has been unable to make full use of its resource treasures. Less than 15 percent of the Soviet Union's population lives there. The northern two-thirds of Siberia are unreachable by road or rail. The North Sea Route has only recently opened the area to large-scale resource extraction and processing.

Clearly, the glory days of Siberia are just beginning. The future can only be better than the tragic past, when Siberia was regarded as a frozen dumping ground for the nation's undesirables. Today Soviet planners foresee a future Siberia of wealthy, bustling towns and cities, sharing the north's wealth with other areas of the nation.

A Different Approach

In the United States and Canada, the basic approach to natural resource use has been to extract minerals or timber from an unpopulated area and then move it long distances for processing and sale. This is not the strategy planned for Siberia. Here the processing and finishing industries are being built at the mines and lumberyards. This creates jobs, which, in turn, attracts permanent settlers. Thus, new cities are born, and people who have moved from Moscow begin to think of themselves as Siberians.

It is hoped that resource use, city building, and industrial growth will be carried out with pollution control in mind. It would indeed be a new tragedy for Siberia if, in a hundred years, the air is murky, the forests chopped down, and the beautiful rivers and mountain ranges ruined.

4

GREAT WHALE RIVER, IN CANADA

Lucy Anoee has not spent the night in an igloo since she was a small girl, caught in a storm with her parents. Her two teenagers, Ernest and Alice, are excited about the experience even though they don't let on to their parents. Their father, Jim Anoee, is searching the snow surface next to the family's two snowmobiles, looking for the right kind of snow to cut into building blocks.

The last time Jim helped build an igloo was with his father, ten years ago. Tonight Jim's parents are snug at home in their wood-and-metal shack, snuggling up to the stove to watch television. Perhaps they are a bit worried about their son's family out on the ice of Hudson Bay in the below-zero twilight of an early spring day, 75 miles (121 km) west of their village of Great Whale River.

There is nothing to worry about, however. Jim and Lucy were raised to remember some of the old Inuit ways, and Jim is an experienced hunter and trapper. Besides, before the family set out this morning, Jim's father gave him a lot of good tips for building an igloo.

Jim brought his children out to see him at work hunting seals. Lucy, who used to travel with Jim before the children were born, is glad to be out in the great stillness, away from Great Whale River village.

Soon Jim is instructing Alice and Ernest on the way to build an igloo. First, Jim hands Alice a long knife. He directs her to cut into the deep snow of a drift. Ernest huffs and puffs as he pulls out the 3-foot (1-m)–long, 6-inch (15-cm)–thick blocks of snow she has cut. Their parents then set the 40-pound (18-kg) blocks on edge in a circle.

As Ernest takes a turn cutting out the second layer of blocks, his father shaves the top surface of the bottom layer, so that the blocks are laid in a sturdy spiral. The second layer of blocks is placed leaning inward to form a curved wall. Each level leans farther in toward the center, and soon, to the teenagers' surprise, a neat little dome-shaped hut sits before them.

It is now that the tips Jim learned from his father reveal the genius of this building method. The squared-off hole that Ernest and Alice excavated the blocks from is at the edge of the igloo. Once it is roofed over, it creates a snug, below-surface tunnel entrance to the igloo. The floor of the igloo is also dug out so that it is below the surface of the snow outside. This provides more protection against the wind.

Lucy is completing the task of fitting the final small blocks together at the top of the dome, leaving a small hole for ventilation. She fills in holes between blocks with loose snow, so the wind won't whistle through. She wants her children to remember this experience positively. It is hopeless to expect them to return to the old Inuit ways, but maybe they can have both old and new in their lives.

The young people crawl in, grumbling. A warm glow greets them. Their father has spread the floor with caribou robes and lit a stove to boil water for tea. "Your granddad threw out the last seal-oil lamp last year," he said, "so we'll have to make do with this modern monster." He pats their battery-powered lantern affectionately.

Tonight the Anoee family eats fish the old way, boiled on their stove. No one complains. The igloo is comfortable and almost warm, just above freezing. The snowmobiles are parked against the igloo, out of the wind. Snug in their sleeping bags and blankets, the family sleeps well.

THE PLACE

The next morning, the Anoee family turns east toward home, traveling steadily across the sometimes smooth, sometimes jagged surface of the sea ice. They are looking for ringed seals, which are emerging to sun themselves in the weak spring sunshine. The seal that Jim shot the day before is their only catch, however. It will provide them with a skin to use or sell and a lot of meat to eat. Ernest and Alice return home with a good story to tell their friends.

By early afternoon the village of Great Whale River is in sight. Situated on the southeast shore of Hudson Bay in northern Canada, the village of Great Whale River is located a few miles south of the treeline boundary. The tree line runs sharply northeast from the east coast of Hudson Bay. However, the only trees visible around the village are those down in the sheltered valley of the Great Whale River. North of the village one may see a 4-foot (120-cm)–tall spruce bravely clinging to a rock every mile or so, but before many miles go by, there's not one tree,

only the gray, orange, and red lichens covering the granite rocks. One advantage to having no trees and no swampy muskeg is that mosquitoes don't breed very well, and those that do survive can't take the wind. North of the treeline, tundra stretches to the edge of frozen islands and seas and beyond them to the permanent ice pack that surrounds the North Pole.

The Canadian North is almost 2,000 miles (3,200 km) from south to north and from east to west. This beautiful, cold, and treeless land makes up almost one-half of Canada's total area of 3,851,809 square miles (9,976,139 sq km). To the south of the treeline, the dark taiga forest is filled with cold ponds, lakes, and rivers. Farmlands and cities are today found mostly in a 200-mile (320-km)–wide strip of Canada just north of the U.S. border.

Plants and Animals of the North

The plants and animals of the Great Whale River area are similar to those already discussed for eastern Siberia and northern Alaska. The northernmost trees are larch and white and black spruce. Farther east are beautiful parklands in which single candelabra spruce stand widely separated on a deep carpet of mosses. North of the treeline the vegetative cover depends on the severity of the weather. Along Hudson Bay one may find reindeer moss, grasses, and some berry plants. Beautiful flowers are scattered across the tundra in the summer.

The big animals of the forest include moose, elk, and caribou. There were once perhaps as many as 5 million of the elegant caribou, roaming the plains and wood-

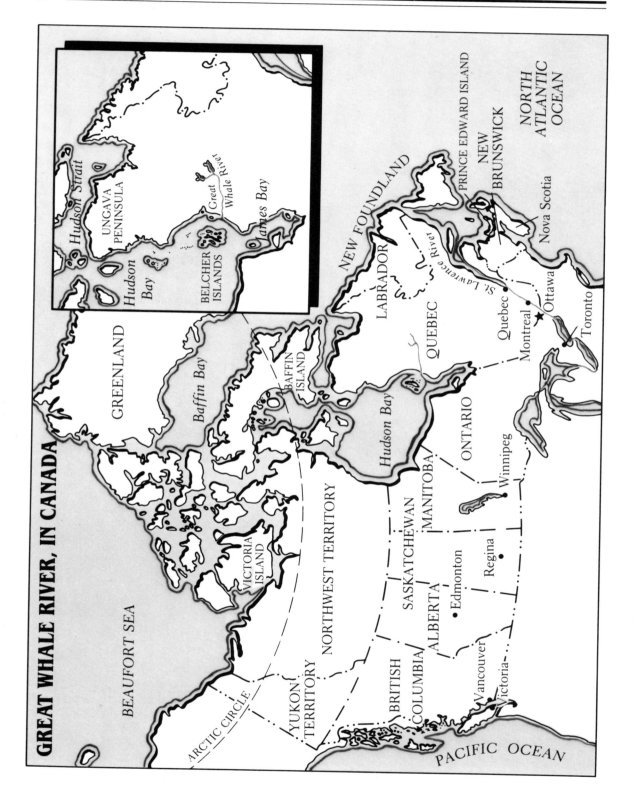

GREAT WHALE RIVER, IN CANADA

*It can be cozy inside an igloo,
as it is for this family.*

*A native northern Canada family moving
over the tundra in the summer*

Polar bears crossing the frozen ice

lands in huge herds. Today, east of Hudson Bay, they are recovering from near *extinction* through overhunting.

There are also many kinds of geese, ducks, and wading birds, making use of all the surface water. On the tundra one may find the lemming, orange ground squirrel, ptarmigan, snowy owl, white fox, wolf, and the giant shaggy muskox. Tiniest of all, and most numerous, are the millions of mosquitoes and black flies.

Hudson Bay:
The Biggest Thing Around

All life forms are affected by the presence of a bay of salt water 320,000 square miles (828,800 sq km) in area, about 500 miles (800 km) across in any direction, and only about 500 feet (152 m) deep.

Some scientists suggest that Hudson Bay was formed when the *continental glaciers* covered this area more than eight thousand years ago. Up to 2 miles (3.2 km) thick, the ice was so heavy that it pressed down the surface of the earth. When the glaciers retreated north, this giant bowl filled up with salt water from the Atlantic Ocean rushing in through what is now named Hudson Strait.

The broad, unusually precise curve of the shore near Great Whale has led some scientists to believe that this may be the eastern rim of the greatest meteorite crater visible on the surface of Earth. The diameter of this possible crater exceeds 350 miles (568 km). The Belcher Islands, made largely of iron ore, sit about in the middle of the crater. Many smaller (and proved) meteorite craters lie throughout the Ungava Peninsula, but none approaches the immensity of this possible one.

Many animals live on and under the sea ice that covers Hudson Bay most of the year. The most spectacular of these are polar bears, which dislike the warmth of summer. These animals may sleep in shallow holes for weeks, waiting for the return of cold weather and firm ice. Their idea of the good life is a cold winter swim among the ice floes, hunting for ringed seal, walrus, whales, and fish. There are more than half a million ringed seals alone in Hudson Bay.

There is more precipitation in the Great Whale River area than in either Barrow, Alaska, or Cherskiy, in eastern Siberia. Long, snowy winters are typical of both forests and open tundra. Summer is not very warm, with many sudden storms. The presence of Hudson Bay contributes to a cold, windy, moist climate.

THE NATIVE PEOPLE

Henry Hudson, an English explorer who discovered the bay in 1610, was marooned there by a mutiny of his ship's crew. The Bay was "discovered" only as far as England and Europe were concerned. The Inuit and Indians who lived along its shores had known about it for thousands of years.

In the late 1660s and 1670s, the first fur-hunting English representatives of the Hudson's Bay Company found that the shores of the bay were well populated. The southern shores of Hudson Bay and James Bay were occupied by Algonkian and Chippewayan Indians, great explorers of the northern woods. Caribou Inuit inhabited the lands west of the bay. The Ungava Inuit were spread from the east coast of the bay across the Ungava Peninsula to Ungava Bay. Where tundra met woods, they traded with the Cree Indians.

Ungava and Cree

The descendants of the Ungava Inuit and Cree Indians live in Great Whale River today. Their history became tangled with that of the British and French explorers who settled in what is today Canada's province of Quebec.

In the past the Ungava Inuit and Cree Indians traveled in small bands of a few families. They moved with the seasons from one camp to another. But they were separated by several important differences. For one thing, they spoke different languages. Also, the Ungava used the natural resources of the tundra and sea ice; the Cree lived off the great woods.

In fact, the Ungava had more in common with the Inuit of Alaska and Siberia, thousands of miles away, than they did with their neighbors, the Cree. Similarly, the Cree had more in common with the Indian tribes of what is today the United States than they did with their tundra-dwelling neighbors.

How They Used the Land

What were some of the differences between the lives of those who knew how to live on the tundra and those who could live in the woods and tundra borderlands? One way to understand the difference is to contrast their *material cultures*. For one

thing, the Ungava lived in domed snow houses during the winter, of the same shape as those described for northern Alaska. The Cree lived in teepees of hide and brush, with a framework of wooden poles. They were using the forest's materials. The Ungava used caribou hide for clothing: parkas, trousers, socks, and boots. There was room in the woman's parka to carry a baby against her back. The Ungava also wore snow goggles made of wood or ivory, with narrow eye slits to protect them from the blinding white glare. The Cree men wore breechcloths and moccasins in warm weather. In colder weather they added a robe, leggings, and buckskin shirt. Women wore long dresses of hides, knee-length leggings, and moccasins.

Not surprisingly, the Ungava carried water, food, and other belongings in bags of hide, as that was all they had. Some dishes were carved from wood, but this was not a plentiful material. The Cree, on the other hand, used birch bark, which they sewed into bags and boxes to carry water, berries, meat, and so on.

The Ungava ate the sea mammals of shore and bay, just as their relatives in Alaska and Siberia did. After seals, walrus, and whales, next in importance were caribou and fish. Much of this heavy meat diet was consumed raw, as there was not much fuel for cooking. Spears and harpoons were the Ungava's major hunting tools. The Cree hunted the woodland caribou, moose, beaver, porcupine, deer, rabbit, and fish. They used spears and bows and arrows. They collected some berries and other wild plants; neither group farmed.

*An Inuit fisherman
hauling in his catch*

Language, Spiritual Belief, Marriage, Work

The Ungava spoke the same language as their distant cousins of Alaska and Siberia, while the Cree would have been understood by Indians south of Lake Michigan.

Both groups believed that humans and animals had souls and that the world was full of powerful spirits. Animals had to be hunted and killed according to a set of rules. If an animal were killed improperly, its soul would inform the living animals that its hunter had been unkind, and then that hunter would be unable to catch any more animals.

Among the Ungava, infants often were betrothed or promised to each other, to marry when they grew older. The uncertainty of life meant that many of these arrangements fell through. Generally, marriage and divorce were somewhat informal. For the Cree, a young man would often offer himself in service to his future father-in-law. For a certain period the older man would test the younger man's skills before allowing him to marry his daughter.

Until very recently, most cultures around the world have practiced a *division of labor* in which certain jobs were done by men, others by women. Among the Ungava and the Cree, men did the hunting and fighting, and women made the clothing, prepared skins for use, did the cooking, and reared the children. Boys learned hunting skills from their fathers, and girls learned household skills from their mothers. It is only recently that men and women around the world have begun to share some tasks.

From this simple set of comparisons, one can see that the Ungava and Cree had some *cultural traits* in common. Other traits were different for the two groups, because different materials and resources were available on the tundra and in the forest.

Recent History of Great Whale River

From the 1660s to 1713, Hudson Bay was the focus of fur hunting and trading by French and English adventurers. Ships were anchored in the bay, and furs caught by the natives were traded for metal kettles, knives, guns, hatchets, and other new items. By 1770 traders had moved into the lands west of the bay. When a region of the New World ran out of its fur-bearing animals, the Europeans moved farther west, leaving behind them Indian and Inuit groups who had become reliant on European trade goods, foods, and alcohol.

In 1857 a permanent trading post was opened by the Hudson's Bay Company at the present site of Great Whale River. By the late nineteenth century, the village was a regional center. Two missionaries and their wives worked to bring Christianity to the Inuit and Cree who moved to the town.

In the winter months the Cree families moved to camps inland, while the Inuit went to their old grounds along the coast. Both groups moved back to the village of Great Whale River in the summer, to trade the furs they had accumulated for

A Hudson Bay town

food and other goods. The village also became the central site for religious and social activities.

Great Whale River functioned as a retreat for the Cree people. After obtaining guns in the seventeenth century, the Cree had expanded their territory to include much of western Canada. They were eventually stopped by resistance from other tribes and by two smallpox epidemics in 1784 and 1838. After these disasters, the Cree were a scattered and demoralized group, living in many widely separated communities across northern Canada.

There were lean decades for the Indian and Inuit, as the North was depleted of its wild game staples and as the market for fur declined. Both the whites and the natives took part in this overkill. The newly introduced guns made the job so easy that more animals were killed than could be used. Only in recent decades, with careful management planning, have the beaver, moose, caribou, and other animals begun to recover in numbers.

Other aspects of Inuit and Indian culture have been greatly affected by the arrival of white ways of life. Most Indians and Inuit now live in settled communities. Few of them know enough of the traditional ways to survive in the wild.

Many natives have moved to one location or another in search of work. When that work runs out, a family is often stuck with no place to go and no money coming in except for welfare payments. As in Alaska and Siberia, transport between distant towns is via airplane. The Canadian North has little ground-based transportation other than snowmobiles, so a poor family has no convenient way of moving to a location with better opportunities.

Another problem in the isolated northern villages is that the center of government is so far away. The capital of Canada, Ottawa, is about 800 air miles (1,288 km) south of Great Whale River. Not much closer is Quebec City, provincial capital for Great Whale River. Most of the 24 million people of Canada can spare little time to think about the problems of their northern citizens. Canadian interests remain focused on the narrow, densely populated strip of territory along the U.S. border.

GREAT WHALE RIVER TODAY

Present-day Great Whale River is not a beautiful place. Running east–west through the center of the village is an airplane landing strip. South of it lies "the Village," where most of the one thousand Inuit and Cree Indians live, separated into two neighborhoods.

To the north of the landing strip is "the Hill." Here the English-speaking and French-speaking Canadian residents of Great Whale River live in the buildings of an old radar base and in newer housing.

Over the past twenty years, Great Whale River has become a regional administrative center for both the Canadian and the Quebec governments. This has meant a great increase in the number of English and French Canadians living there. It also has meant that the native people have been exposed to the culture of southern Canada and have had better

Houses in the Arctic must be built on stilts to avoid melting the permafrost.

access to medical care, education, and improved housing.

The older shacks of the Inuit and the canvas huts of the Cree have been almost completely replaced by wooden frame and prefabricated housing. Like the Nageak family in Barrow, the Anoee family lives in a new home among the other Inuit families. Jim Anoee's parents are traditionalists, however, and see no need to move out of their wood-and-metal shack. Jim's dad even keeps a dog team, which he uses mostly when his snowmobile breaks down.

This happens often enough to justify the effort involved in catching fish for the dogs.

The approximately six hundred Inuit settled in their neighborhood of the village originally came from several different places along Hudson and James bays. Their lives are significantly better than in the lean years earlier in the century.

The Inuit have modern housing and oil heat. Many have electricity, telephones, and a variety of up-to-date appliances. Some of the Inuit have regular wage-paying jobs. Most of the Inuit families supplement the money they have by hunting for food in a semitraditional fashion. Snowmobiles and guns have replaced dogsleds and harpoons, but seal meat, caribou, and fish are still valued foods. Some Inuit bring in a little money by carving in stone and ivory. Government assistance remains essential for survival, however. Inuit community members are local political leaders. They are increasingly involved in decision-making at the provincial and federal levels of Canadian government. Some experts feel that the Inuit of Great Whale River village have adjusted well to modern life.

What of the approximately four hundred Cree residents? As with the Inuit, many Cree have found wage work. Few of them maintain completely their traditional forest culture. However, they add to their income and government welfare payments with some hunting and fishing.

As with the Inuit, the social lives of the Cree revolve around their group. They are beginning to have a greater say in local politics. Generally, the Cree have a lower status than the Inuit. Government decisions have in the past tended to favor the Inuit over the Cree.

Both native groups have given up their traditional spiritual beliefs for membership in the Anglican Church. They attend church regularly and abide by the teachings taught to them by past and present missionaries.

The two native groups have learned to interact more with one another and to speak English. However, there are still enough cultural divisions and tensions be-

tween the Inuit and Cree to prevent their working together for a better future.

The four groups of Great Whale River remain separated in their various parts of town. The tension among them can be seen partly in the fact that each group calls the settlement by a different name. The official Quebec name is *Poste de la Baleine* (Whale Station), but the English-speaking Canadians call it Great Whale River. In the Inuit language (Inukitut), the name for their part of the settlement is *Kuujjuaapik* (whale of the sea). The Cree Indians tend to use the French name of *Pointe au Sable* (black sable) for their village on the "wrong side" of the airstrip. When notices appear on bulletin boards or are read over the radio, the words reflect the social status of each group. For example, when an aircraft is about to land or take off, people are warned not to cross the airstrip by a loud bell, a flashing yellow light, and a sign that warns of the danger: first in French, then in English, then in Inuktitut for the Inuit, and finally, in Cree. The Cree Indians are continually reminded that they're at the bottom of the social standing at *Poste de la Baleine,* Quebec.

The white community in Great Whale River runs most of the government institutions that affect the natives. The federal school is probably the point of most contact between the groups. Many of the southern Canadians who come to Great Whale River are not trained to deal with another culture. As a result, they often see the behavior of the natives in a negative way, as inferior to that of the whites. These attitudes must change if

Canadian natives are to participate in deciding their own future.

PAST AND PRESENT ATTEMPTS AT RESOURCE DEVELOPMENT

Many changes have already come to the southern Hudson Bay region, especially along James Bay. These changes have been both good and bad for the residents of Great Whale River and the other small settlements along Hudson Bay.

In the mid-1950s hundreds of Inuit people from the north and Cree Indians from the forests south of Great Whale River were brought to this site on the shore of Hudson Bay to help build the Mid-Canada Line's radar stations. This was part of the Distant Early Warning System (DEW-Line), built to warn North America of possible bomber attacks over the North Pole from the Soviet Union. Before long, new missiles were developed. These missiles traveled at such high speeds that the Mid-Canada Line's few minutes of warning were useless. As a result, all the bases closed down, and military operations ended in 1967. Since there was no place for the Inuit and Indians to go for work, the Quebec and federal governments allowed them to remain in Great Whale River, living primarily on welfare payments.

Many of the Inuit had been brought from Rankin Inlet and other northern places where mines had been closed, so this was the second time they had been promised a great deal by technology and then left disappointed.

During the 1970s the Quebec provincial government decided to harness the waters of its northern lands to generate electricity for sale to cities far to the south. Quebec and its Ungava Peninsula have other resources, including iron, lead, and zinc, but *hydroelectric power* offers the best return. The development plan was first known as the James Bay Project, but is now called *La Grande Complex*. It called for damming up some of the greatest rivers flowing west out of the Quebec wilderness into James Bay.

If put together, the dams and associated levees would stretch a total of 130 miles (208 km). Holding back huge lakes, the dam operators would release controlled amounts of water into turbines to generate electricity at low cost for use by southern Canada and New England cities. The electricity generated by the turbines was carried in five high-voltage cables slung from twelve thousand transmission towers stretching south to the great cities.

Planners of a new and greater Quebec (Nouveau Québec) hope also to attract industries into northern Quebec. This would lead to greater development of the Ungava's other natural resources and provide permanent work and a higher quality of life for the northern natives.

Results of Development Plans

On the negative side, the giant dams, levees, and lakes of *La Grande Complex* have ruined thousands of square miles where the Cree Indians have hunted and trapped for three thousand years. The James Bay Agreement between the Quebec

A hydroelectric plant

government and the native groups attempts to repay the Inuit and Cree for loss of their traditional lands.

The natives agreed to give up all claims in the future to all resources in northern Quebec for a payment of money and the use of some lands. The Cree were given $135 million; the Inuit, $90 million. Between them the two groups kept ownership of 5,400 square miles (14,040 sq km). In addition, they were given permanent hunting and fishing rights to 60,000 square miles (155,000 sq km). The government also agreed to hire natives first for any construction work or other jobs developed in the north.

The people at Great Whale River were pleased to be able to work for about six years on *La Grande Complex* and to earn large salaries—up to five hundred dollars per week for unskilled labor. Everything seemed wonderful during those few years, but now what? The great dams and electricity-generating stations can be run by just a few workers, so the promise of jobs remains unfulfilled. And dreams of northern industrial centers remain dreams.

Even worse, part of the grand plan is to add eventually a dam on the Great Whale River. Again there'll be high-paying jobs for several years. One very likely result of this additional development activity will be that the settlement at Great Whale River will have to be moved. Will the Inuit and Cree go with it, perhaps farther north?

New Native-Run Lands: Is It Possible?

Perhaps soon there may be a new kind of opportunity. To the west and north of

Hudson Bay lie the vast Northwest Territories of Canada. The natives of this area of 1,300,000 square miles (3,367,000 sq km) are dissatisfied with the present government and want to create a new one. The native peoples want to divide the Northwest Territories into two new territories, the Inuit one to be called Nunavut ("our land"), the Indian one, Denendeh ("our land").

The Canadian government must approve such a division, of course, but it has said it's ready to accept the general idea. Because Indians prefer hunting and living in the woods, and Inuit prefer the open spaces, one suggestion is that the present Northwest Territories be divided approximately along the North American treeline. This would give all lands north and east of that line to the new Inuit territory, Nunavut, and all lands to the west and south to the Indian territory, Denendeh.

Another suggestion is that the division be along the northerly extension of the present boundary between Manitoba and Saskatchewan up to the North Pole, with all to the east of that line going to make up Nunavut, all to the west going to the Indian Denendeh. The government has said that the native peoples must first decide where that line of division will be, and then the government will discuss further the details of such a division.

Many of the natives hope that eventually each territory will become a province, to gain votes in Canada's parliamentary government. The matter is not a simple one, considering the huge amounts of minerals, oil, and gas now under exploration throughout northern Canada. How much money should the new native territories receive from these resources? Should it be done as it was under the Alaska Native Claims Settlement Act? Or is there some other way that will be fair to all groups involved?

Because Great Whale River is not in the Northwest Territories, what effect might the nearby presence of two native-run territories have on those Inuit and Indians living in Great Whale? Would some or all of the Inuit want to return to their native lands? If the Indians wanted to move to Denendeh, would the Cree be accepted by the western Chippewayan tribes? If monies are to be paid to the new territories by the Canadian federal government, would the natives receive any, especially if they had already received some as the result of the James Bay Agreement with the Cree and Inuit of Quebec? Many questions remain, but progress is being made toward fairness for the natives.

5

A COMPARISON OF THREE POLAR REGIONS: THE NORTH IS ALIVE

In this book you have examined the way of life of some of the peoples who live in the Arctic: the Inuit and white societies in northern Alaska, the Yakaghir and Russian society of eastern Siberia, and the four-culture complexity of a village on the shore of Canada's Hudson Bay. You have found that this cold cap on the earth is alive with people and their activities, and other forms of life.

PEOPLES OF THE NORTH

In all three locations, there are two layers of human residents. The native peoples—Inuit, Yakaghir, and Cree—came to the cold lands centuries ago. They developed ways of earning a living from a land frozen ten months of the year. They learned to use nature's resources for food, as building materials, and for clothing. They also developed unique means of transport. Finally, they had a lively social and spiritual life. Perhaps the greatest challenge these groups have had to face was the arrival of white society.

Of the groups making up the second layer of human residents—Americans, Soviets, and Canadians—all three see the Arctic as a frozen frontier. They see it as an empty land filled with opportunities to develop personal and national wealth. Are these people up to the challenge? Can they do as well as the natives? Can modern-day technology adapt to arctic conditions without destroying the land and people?

This book has said a lot about how modern technology has been responsible for rapid change among the North's native peoples. Until recently, these technological tools were used only to extract resources and transport them far away. Now governments are beginning to think in terms of developing the North itself. If this takes place, the native peoples may finally find themselves totally in the modern world.

FURS, WHALES, AND GOLD

Furs and skins first brought whites into the circumpolar lands. The Russians traded for furs with native Alaskans and Siberians; the English and French moved into the great untapped region of Hudson Bay.

The native Inuit of Alaska had their first encounters with white men in the 1800s, when vessels from Nantucket and other Massachusetts ports came up through the Bering Strait looking for whales. No one could have believed at the time that the white men's new tools for hunting whales would soon almost wipe out the seemingly endless whale population. A large element of the natives' food supply was being destroyed just to supply oil for lamps and baleen for corsets.

Natural resources are never static. As fashions changed in the southern regions, there was less demand for furs, skins, and baleen from the north. Gold was discovered in the Yukon Territory of Canada in 1898 and soon after in the gravel of Nome, Alaska. As the gold became more difficult for individuals to find with their gold-panning techniques, more and more modern equipment was moved into the Far North. Today most of these giant machines lie rusting away on the worked-out gravel of the Klondike and Yukon rivers in Canada's Yukon Territory. Gold mining is still extremely important in arctic eastern Siberia. The world's largest above-ground and underground deposits of gold may be in the mountains near the southern reaches of the Kolyma River.

Other minerals have been discovered in the Arctic and have been transported out of the region, south. Seldom have the activities surrounding the mining or harvesting of natural resources led to the long-range betterment of the northern native peoples. For a while their lives seem better with the new jobs and income, and then it all stops, often abruptly. Sometimes the activity stops because the people of the south decide they no longer want that resource. At other times the activity slows and then stops simply because there are no more minerals worth mining. At still other times a new invention in the south makes a mineral or other resource no longer useful.

No one worries about what the decision to stop production means to the lives of the native peoples; the southerners simply "fold their tents" and go home. Meanwhile, during years of working in the mines or forests, a generation or two of natives has grown up without learning the traditional ways of surviving off the sea and the land. For the Inuit of Alaska, Canada, Greenland, and Norway, this has often led to their being given welfare payments by their governments.

IN THE CANADIAN AND U.S. ARCTIC

In the Canadian and U.S. Arctic, once the oil and gas wells have been drilled, the dams built, and the pipelines laid, there will be few jobs necessary to keep things flowing. What will the Inuit and Indian workers then do? Would they ever want to return to the old ways? Faced with no income from gas or oil, would these people, who have "tasted the good life," agree to return to lower standards of living? Would they, instead, migrate south to become part of the white peoples' cultures? Would their ancient cultures gradually die out if this happens? Much of the old culture already has been lost to the technological and cultural invasions from the south. Could traditional ways be expected to withstand continued pressure over another generation? Or will North America's Arctic natives use their temporary wealth to create a great new native-run nation at the top of the world?

IN THE ARCTIC REGIONS OF THE SOVIET UNION

The Soviet government believes that its method of developing frontier lands works better than the United States's and Canada's. The Soviets claim that Canada and the United States go into an underdeveloped region like the Arctic and remove natural resources for use far away. The North Americans, the Soviets charge, make no serious attempt to improve the region where the resources were discovered. The Soviets claim their method is to use the resources of a region to develop that region economically and culturally. Using this method, the Soviets have created many new cities in the Far North with populations of ten thousand, fifty thousand, and one hundred thousand or more.

The rest of the north circumpolar world has almost no cities of such size. Fairbanks and Anchorage, Alaska, and Magadan, USSR, are large northern cities, but are not truly arctic. If we were to speak only of cities north of the Arctic Circle, the Soviet Union has all the cities with more than ten thousand people. The Soviet Union has large plans and projects underway to develop completely its northern regions; the United States and Canada have no plans for developing their northern lands as yet.

Those who do not live in the Arctic should be concerned about the way it is used. Its native peoples have been changed by the introduction of white culture. Sometimes these changes have been for the better. Sometimes they have been for the worse. Will the natural environment of the Arctic—animals, birds, plants, mountains, lakes, and air—be changed for the worse in the name of progress?

Once Americans thought *their* land was limitless. All too soon they overused many of its resources, and now must be very careful to save those that still exist. Will North Americans and Soviets see that development of the new Arctic frontier goes hand-in-hand with protection of its people and environment?

GLOSSARY

Anthropologist—a scientist who studies the origin, physical makeup, and culture of human beings.

Archaeologist—a scientist who reconstructs the past by studying remains of houses, clothing, bones, and other objects left by past peoples.

Arctic—the north polar region of the earth.

Arctic Circle—a parallel of latitude at 66½ degrees north.

Baleen—bonelike material, which some whales have instead of teeth, used to strain food from water.

Collective farm—a state-owned farm in which the land, equipment, and herds are owned by the state; each farmer or herder is allowed to farm a small plot or herd a few animals for personal use.

Communism—an economic system in which the government owns the natural resources and factories and determines prices.

Continental glacier—a large mass of flowing ice, covering an area of several thousand square miles.

Cossack—a southern Russian who was a member of the cavalry under the tsars.

Culture—a way of life devised by people for getting along with the environment and each other.

Culture trait—a belief, idea, or way of behavior typical of members of a particular ethnic group.

Dissident—one who openly disagrees with authority.

Division of labor—assignment of certain tasks to certain groups within a family or culture group.

Ecologist—a scientist who studies the relationships among living things and their environment.

Environment—the physical features of the world around us.

Ethnic—belonging to a particular cultural group.

Extinction—elimination of a plant or animal species.

Hydroelectric power—electricity generated by allowing water to fall through a turbine, usually at a dam.

Inuit—the native peoples of North Alaska, also known as the Eskimo.

Keratin—a flexible substance that makes up hair and horn.

Material culture—the objects used by a culture group, including tools, clothing, buildings, etc.

Model—a simplification of the real thing.

Muskeg—stunted coniferous forest found in swampy circumpolar areas.

Nomad—a person who moves among several locations rather than living permanently at one site.

Permafrost—soil that is frozen all year round.

Polar region—the cold belt of land that rings the North and South poles.

Precipitation—water that falls as rain, snow, sleet, or hail.

Region—an area within which elements of culture or environment are similar.

Taiga—coniferous forest typical of areas of cold climate.

Technikum—technical training school in the USSR.

Topography—shape of the land surface, including mountains, valleys, etc.

Tree line—boundary zone separating forest and tundra.

Tributary—a river or stream that flows into a larger river.

Tsar—the ruler of Russia before the 1917 revolution.

Tundra—an area of low, grassy vegetation found in very cold climates.

Umiak—Inuit boat made of skin and used in whaling and walrus hunting.

Yakaghir—ethnic group occupying northeastern Siberia along the Kolyma River.

Yaranga—large, teepee-shaped tent made of reindeer skins by the Yakaghir of Siberia.

FOR FURTHER READING

Cheney, Theodore A. Rees. *Land of the Hibernating Rivers*. New York: Harcourt Brace Jovanovich, 1967.

Fordham, Derek. *Eskimos*. Morristown, NJ: Silver Burdett, 1979.

Judge, Joseph. "Peoples of the Arctic." *National Geographic* 163, no. 2(1983): 144–149.

Lavcock, George. *Beyond the Arctic Circle*. New York: Four Winds Press, 1978.

Lengyel, Emil. *Siberia*. New York: Franklin Watts, 1974.

Liversidge, Douglas. *The First Book of the Arctic*. New York: Franklin Watts, 1967.

Mowat, Farley. *Canada North*. Boston: Little, Brown, 1967.

———. *The Siberians*. Boston: Little, Brown, 1970.

Oswalt, Wendell H. *Eskimos and Explorers*. Novato, CA: Chandler & Sharp, 1979.

Rytkheu, Yuri. "People of the Long Spring." *National Geographic* 163, no. 2(1983): 206–223.

Scullion, Anthony. "How the Experts Build an Igloo." *Canadian Geographic* 101, no. 5(1981): 52–53.

Smith, Thomas G. "How Inuit Trapper-Hunters Make Ends Meet." *Canadian Geographic* 99, no. 3(1980): 56–61.

Taylor, J. Garth. "Trying to Preserve Our Aboriginal Cultures." *Canadian Geographic* 100, no. 6(1980): 52–58.

Vesilind, Priit J. "Hunters of the Lost Spirit." *National Geographic* 163, no. 2(1983): 150–173.

INDEX

ABOUT THE AUTHOR

The author had his interest in polar affairs first whetted in the eighth grade when he had to write a book report about *Alone* by antarctic explorer Admiral Richard E. Byrd. Only five years later, while the author was in the U.S. Navy, he became yeoman to the admiral on Byrd's final expedition to Antarctica. The next year, as yeoman to Commodore Quackenbush, he took part in an expedition that took his icebreaker farther north than any ship had ever gone in one season.

Out of the navy, Mr. Cheney earned a degree in geology and a master's degree in geography. Some years later, he conducted environmental analyses on the western shore of Hudson Bay, Canada, for Cornell University. These and later trips to Alaska and Great Whale River on the eastern shore of Hudson Bay led the author in 1967 to write a book about ecosystems of the arctic, *Land of the Hibernating Rivers*. Twenty years later, he found life for people living in polar regions so dramatically changed that he felt he had to write this new book.

Professor Cheney, now director of the writing program at Fairfield University, had also published *Camping by Backpack and Canoe*; *Day of Fate*; *Getting the Words Right*; and *Writing Creative Nonfiction*.